G000126234

REMEMBERING
ASHFORD

STEVE R. SALTER

The
History
Press

Dedicated to Mum, Dad and James

Mum – Lyn Salter

It is with regret that in 2007, my darling Mum Lyn Salter was diagnosed with Vascular Dementia. It has been a difficult time for myself and my family, and after a long illness, we were all devastated and shocked to find that Mum is suffering from this degenerative disease.

To many of those people who know me personally through my local history research, you will know how close I am to my Mum. She was always so supportive and so proud that I fulfilled my lifetime ambition to write about my home town and I am glad that she was able to celebrate with me my last four titles. I would like to thank everyone for their overwhelming support and kind words during this difficult time, and find it only fitting that I place a special dedication to my Mum, whom I miss so much, and cherish the time that I still have with her.

With love always Mum. Thanks for everything

Steve xxxxx

With special dedication to the memory of Ian Stanley Gambrill (4 April 1947– 8 January 2009). 'An astounding photographer, originally trained with the Weaver brothers, eventually excelling with Countrywide Photographic for over 30 years, and latterly Reflections.' A gentleman whose memory deserves to and will live on. The kindness from both Ian and his wife, Sue, has allowed me to fulfill my childhood dream.

A pleasure to have known you Ian.

Steve R. Salter, March 2009

First published 2009

The History Press
The Mill, Brimscombe Port
Stroud, Gloucestershire, GL5 2QG
www.thehistorypress.co.uk

ISBN 978 07509 4968 2

Printed in Great Britain

CONTENTS

ACKNOWLEDGEMENTS

Over the years many local people and companies have been extremely kind and patient in assisting me with my research. Many have given me very valuable information, which has enabled me to put together an interesting record of the history of Ashford and to build up a substantial photographic collection.

I am overwhelmed by the continued support for and the huge success of *Changing Ashford, Ashford Then and Now, Ashford 1950–1980* and *Around Ashford*. I am also very grateful to those who have followed my fortunes over the past twenty-four years. Without their kindness, this book wouldn't be possible. As always, I have received much generosity from individuals and organisations that have readily allowed me to use their pictures. I would therefore like to give special thanks to the following:

James Adams; Richard Filmer and Pauline Cooper, Halifax Estate Agents; Peter and Pam Goodwin; Jim Ashby and Mrs Joan Ashby; Howard and Christine Green; Allan and Lynn Ward; Mike Bennett, Alistair Irvine, Dave Downey, Gary Browne, Kent Messenger Group – Ashford; John and Val Williams; Ben Grabham, Ray Wilkinson and Pam Herrapath at Ashford Borough Council; ITV Meridian; Waterstone's; W.H. Smith; Maureen Apps and staff at Sussex Stationers; Massimo and Mauro Deidda and Justyna Jaworska; Brian Badham; Vivienne Kenny; Sylvia and Sid Marsh; Betty Shadwell; Cllr Rita Hawes; Richard Warnock-Horn at Laing O'Rourke; Cllr Allen and Mrs Christine Wells; Cllr Palma and Mr Frankie Laughton; Stanhope Parish Council; David Worsley; Valerie Snell (née Hayward); Jo-Ann Baxter; Ashford School; Lyn Sumner; Tony Houps; Ian and Sue Gambrill – www.reflections-images.co.uk (Weavers/Countrywide Archive); Rob Waters; A-C Video; Gloria and Alan Lavender; John Kennedy; Montserrat Clavaguera; Chrissie Rundle, Tim Gregory and Brian McNaughton at Premier Foods; Mr and Mrs Keith Brown; Steve Pepe at Kall-Kwik Ashford; Jon Barrett; Kevin Brown and staff at Snappy Snaps Ashford; Rita Deverill and Bernard Button; Melanie Pentecost; Paul Cook at Dukelease Properties (London); Ufuk Shen, proprietor of Café Express; Stella Pitt; Terry and Christine Baker; June, Ashford Library; Su Berry.

I would also like to express my gratitude as chairman of Ashford History Forum to the ever-faithful David Geoghegan at Kent County Council, and to County Councillors George Koowaree and Derek Smyth for their monetary contribution to this publication and the continuing works of the forum. Also, I owe a big thank you to Cllr Palma Laughton and Stanhope Parish Council for their monetary contribution towards this publication. Your generosity is very much appreciated. As always a big thank you to Ian and Sue Gambrill, who hold the copyright to all Weavers and Countrywide images, many of which can be ordered on the internet at www.reflections-images.co.uk. Many thanks to you both for your continued support.

Thanks are also due to anyone whose name has not been acknowledged here, either through an oversight or because the original source or present ownership of pictures is unknown or unavailable.

And lastly, as always I owe thanks to Michelle Tilling at The History Press for her continued support and, above all, patience.

INTRODUCTION

The face of our town, Ashford, today is a far cry from what the town once was. Previously described as a 'sleepy market town', the expansion of Ashford in recent years has given the town a new identity, a new lease of life and has many an attraction for newcomers to the town. Every town of any size in Britain has its ups and downs, and there is no hiding that Ashford hasn't escaped in this area, especially at the hands of 'unsympathetic developers'. In recent years, this stance has been the subject of much reversal, which again has been subject to mixed opinions on many issues from locals.

For example, the infamous ring road received its makeover back in 2007, in an attempt to claim back the town's lost neighbours, by means of a 'shared space' scheme trialled in Holland. Nearly one year on, work is still in progress at various sections of the scheme, but the finished areas still have major issues. The two-way conversion of the road has caused public outrage among the local people, and many people feel that the road had been put back to its original layout of pre-1974, which nowadays is causing 'gridlock', plus there are many more vehicles on the road in 2008. One has to give praise to the local authorities for attempting to 'right the wrongs' of the past, but a large percentage of Ashfordians would have rather seen the 'Victoria Way' project completed prior to the ring-road project commencing, which would have allowed a diversion for those using the town to get from one side of the A28 to the other.

Elsewhere in the town, the County Square refurbishment and substantial extension has been completed on the former Stanhay site, creating a fresh look on the shopping scene in the town. The design of the new development is perhaps not within keeping with the 'historic' areas of the town, and has probably caused many past historians to 'turn in their graves', but it would be fair to say that the town has gained something that it could have benefited from many years ago.

Another subject, which is personally close to my heart, is Ashford International Station. Back in the late nineties, the local council fought European Passenger Services Limited (now known as Eurostar), to have the high-speed trains to Europe pass through the town, hence having an international station. Ashford won this status and 'Eurostar' has proved to be one of the town's success stories of recent years. But back in 2006, and to come into action upon the opening of Ebbsfleet International in North Kent, an announcement was made to cut the services from Ashford to Paris and Brussels. It wasn't a decision that was taken lightly, and further outrage in the town's history began. Many people were ready to slate Eurostar for their decision, and local newspaper the *Kentish Express* extensively covered stories of unhappy residents. Upon further investigation, it has been highlighted on regular occasions that numbers of passengers travelling from Ashford International were not enough to warrant having the train stop at both Ebbsfleet and Ashford. Even back in 1995, the *Kentish Express* published a supplement upon the opening of the station, which included an independent 'future usage assessment' of the Ashford site commissioned by EPSL, which stated 'if Ashford International is not continuously promoted locally and used to a high capacity, it may fail,' which basically meant 'use it or lose it!' Concerns are still apparent that the facility might close, but Eurostar continually denies any closure. We have yet to see if the future looks bright for Ashford International. One thing to note though is that Eurostar reintroduced its Brussels service on 23 February 2009.

It's not all bad news though, as the previously mentioned redevelopments in the town are destined to be completed by the end of this year, and are said to enhance the character of Ashford, which the town has always retained.

This long-awaited fifth volume is guaranteed to appeal to those who are passionate about their town, and remember the days when things were 'calmer'. *Remembering Ashford* follows on from *Around Ashford* and my previous works, and contains over 300 previously unseen local views spanning the past fifty years. For many of the images, this will be the first time they have been seen; for others, the first time for many years. *Remembering Ashford* continues a fascinating look into a lost, perhaps somewhat changeable era, where expansion and redevelopment was largely yet to take place.

Steve R. Salter
March 2009

1

IDENTITY PARADE

Station Road, 1966. This extremely rare view shows Station Road in its pre-ring road days. Familiar to many, F. Bucknell, confectioner and tobacconist, can be seen on the corner of Station Road and St John's Lane at no. 14, with the Baptist Church just creeping into the extreme right of the picture. Although the Baptist Church still stands today, no. 14 was demolished in 1967 together with its adjacent neighbouring buildings. Vicarage Lane car park now largely covers the site, and, in particular, The Joe Fagg Pop-In Centre stands approximately where this building once stood. (*Bryan Sales*)

Station Road, 1966. Just to the left of the tobacconist stood another two businesses which have also faded into history. Popular ladies hairstylists Betty's stood at no. 16, which at the time was approximately opposite County Market Stores. Another business to fall in the hands of the bulldozer was Universal Photo Service at no. 18. During this era, there were numerous photography outlets in the town, namely Weavers, Studio Photocraft and Peter of Kennington to name but a few. (*Bryan Sales*)

East Hill, 1966. One of many hostelries lost during the early 1970s was the Duke of Marlborough, which stood at the top of East Hill at its junction with Wellesley Road, Station Road and High Street. A popular inn, it was the most attractive building out of those lost at this time. An interesting fact in its history illustrates that the turreted corner was an addition while under repair back in the 1930s. Earlier pictures from the turn of the century show the 'Duke' minus this poignant feature. Replaced with the ring road, members of the Temperance Society thought it to be a fair trade-off; others have been drowning their sorrows ever since. (*Bryan Sales*)

Somerset Road, 1966. This particularly rare view shows Keens Stores at no. 28, which stood alongside the footpath in Somerset Road. This led to Wellesley Road, prior to redevelopment for Charter House in December 1971. The area beyond the Austin A40, parked on the right, was largely the garden to 22 North Street, which in turn was sold to Metropolitan Estates a year after this picture was taken. Subsequently, purchasers Charter Consolidated, who were already occupying an overcrowded Kent House, used the site to construct its new eight-storey office complex, but not without controversy. (*Bryan Sales*)

Park Road, 1966. Many Ashfordians will clearly remember Cherry's grocers which once stood in Park Road, adjacent to the junction of Kent Avenue. One of many traditional traders in the town in those days, Cherry's closed in the early 1970s, later to become the Vacuum Centre before it was finally demolished in 1985 for the Park Mall Shopping Centre. A sign of the times, nowadays you wouldn't think about leaving your child outside a shop in a pushchair or pram. What a sad reminder of the insecurities of life today. (*Bryan Sales*)

Park Road, 1966. Just opposite Cherry's stood Park Road grocer and Post Office, at the time run by G. and M. Wood. The workshops of Hayward's Garage can be seen to the rear of the premises, which were purchased by Caffyn's in 1967. The post office was to be demolished several years later in 1974. Where would all those pensioners go, who are seen congregating outside? It's probably pension day! (*Bryan Sales*)

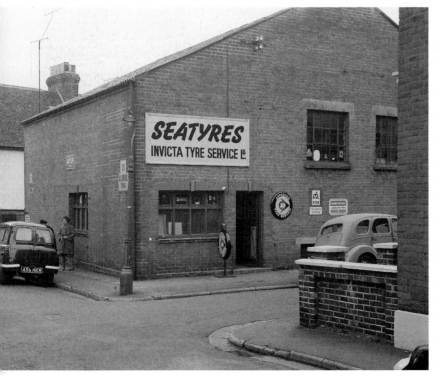

Wolseley Road, 1966. Previously Swoffers wholesale fruiterers' warehouse, Seatyres stood at the junction of Stone Street and Wolseley Road, with Edinburgh Road running to the rear of the premises. By the late 1970s, Seatyres had been demolished together with much of the surrounding business premises and residential property. Charter Consolidated had purchased the site for redevelopment in 1976, and were urged by the council to clear the remaining dwellings in Edinburgh Road as they had fallen into dereliction. Again, this was earmarked for Park Mall. (*Bryan Sales*)

Godinton Road, 1966. Back in the late 1960s this section of Godinton Road, nearest the junction with Bank Street, was littered with many individual traders, a luxury that this area lost in latter years. The Candy Shop and Binney's Antiques can be seen in the foreground at Market Buildings, opposite the then Market Hotel. Further to the left, Tilworth Enterprises Ltd can be seen advertising 'Everything for the handyman'. Their premises stood next door to the familiar Maylam's Restaurant, and were demolished together with the restaurant and a large section of Godinton Road in 1967. This enabled work to get underway for the Tufton Street shopping development. The Candy Shop remains vacant at present and Kent Kebab has occupied the premises of Binney's for the last sixteen years. This section of the street remained a thoroughfare until recently, when it was obliterated by the new County Square extension. (*Bryan Sales*)

Godinton Road, 1966. A fascinating view showing one of the many individual trades that once dominated the lower end of Godinton Road, and are just now a distant memory. The Market Tobacco and Cigar stores at no. 3 stood adjacent to the modelling department of Timbercraft at no. 1, whose splendid neighbouring timber and DIY store at no. 1a, closed as recently as 1993, and was the last of this side of Godinton Road to be demolished, although there had been no urgency to do so. The site now accommodates the new County Square extension, and makes this area totally unrecognisable today. Much of this area had been bulldozed during a ten-year period between 1973 and 1983. (*Bryan Sales*)

Godinton Road, 1966. Another familiar name of the past was Gordon's Newsagent and Tobacconist at 7 Godinton Road, near to the junction of Hempsted Street. Gordon's was approximately opposite Maylam's Restaurant and the Invicta public house, and escaped destruction during the war despite a bomb falling on the nearby premises of Stanhay, resulting in loss of life. (*Bryan Sales*)

Godinton Road, 1966. The premises of W.A. Pike General Stores can be seen here at no. 147. Interestingly, in 1966 the street was not short of trades of this nature, but today it is a different story with only one, namely Mins at no. 157. How times have changed. (*Bryan Sales*)

Godinton Road, 1966. Nowadays more familiar as the ever-popular Mins Stores, no. 157 is seen here as Central Stores. Today almost doubled in size, Mins continues to be a success, being the only general store in a substantial residential area. All this despite various traffic-calming schemes and access only to buses and taxis from the direction of Chart Road. (*Bryan Sales*)

Godinton Road, 1966. It would be fair to say that this street certainly had choice back in the swinging sixties. L.G. Moy, Post Office, Grocer and Provision Merchant, stood at the corner of Eastern Avenue at no. 162, and directly opposite Central Stores. There was much competition to be had at this time. Today Harding's Chartered Surveyors occupy the premises. (*Bryan Sales*)

Godinton Road, 1966. Many motorcycle fans of the day will remember W. Camier's cycle shop and petrol filling station at nos 75–7. The Camier family, locally known for their expertise in the motorcycling world, also had premises at 46a Park Street. More recently, one of the younger generation of the family, Leon, excels locally and nationally in many motorcycling tournaments. Only two of the bay-windowed houses still stand today after Amoco redeveloped the site in the late 1960s for a new filling station. Today the site has been transformed into an Enterprise Rent-a-Car outlet. (*Bryan Sales*)

Godinton Road junction with West Street, 1966. For the last thirty-three years West Street has been identified as the sharp bend of the ring road by the Telephone Exchange, but back in 1966 the street was typical of any in the town. Sadly, it was during the alterations of the early 1970s that it was changed beyond recognition. Works involved numerous dwellings being sacrificed under the Compulsory Purchase laws, and this left the street with hardly any identity. West Street is currently undergoing intensive cosmetic alteration and the sharp one-way bend will soon be no more. (*Bryan Sales*)

Tufton Street, 1966. Prior to the advent of industrial estates on the outskirts of the town centre, many businesses held prime locations within the heart of the town. J.W. Hall & Co., Builders Merchant and Ironmonger, can be seen here a few years before their relocation to Cobbs Wood. Their main shop and trade counters were located in the timber-clad building in the centre, which was at one time a slaughterhouse. The kitchen, bathroom and fireplace showrooms were in the more recent building further up Tufton Street to the left. The older buildings were replaced in the early 1970s by Tufton House, new offices for the Industrial Tribunal and, more recently, Ashford College of Art and Design. The showrooms became offices for the reputable publication, *Dog World*. In recent years, *Dog World* was converted into Spectrum House, a charming residential development. (*Bryan Sales*)

Elwick Road, January 1966. This nostalgic view shows Elwick Road six years prior to its alteration for the ring road. Just behind the trees is Ashford Market, which was made somewhat smaller when the road scheme began. Many Ashfordians will remember the old council Slipper Baths and Public Conveniences, which are just out of view to the left of the two ladies chatting by the old Ford Cortina. Although much altered today, the footbridge to Jemmett Road and South Ashford can be seen (centre), beside the Burrows & Co. billboards. (*Bryan Sales*)

Elwick Road, 1966. Further into the summer months, the market is obscured by the large oak trees, which once graced the perimeter of the site. Today the area is unrecognisable in the absence of the trees, with only a couple left standing. (*Bryan Sales*)

Elwick Road, 1966. This extremely rare view shows the main entrance to the nationally acclaimed Ashford Market, with Elwick Villa to the right, which was once the home of Gerald Brown the greengrocer. Note the white jacket-clad market attendant overseeing the visitors to the market. In 1966 nearby Godinton Road was still a through road to the A20 to Maidstone, as indicated by the road sign. The M20 missing link was yet to be built. (*Bryan Sales*)

Elwick Road, 1966. Another view indicates that the market entrance was something of a meeting point, showing locals chatting as a livestock lorry enters the market. An interesting fact is that this is approximately where the new curved frontage of Debenhams stands today in the new County Square extension. What an astounding difference! (*Bryan Sales*)

Upper High Street, 1966. Many will remember the premises of Dolcis Shoe Co. with its familiar mansard roof at 88–90 High Street. Latterly Curtess Shoes, the property's connection with the shoe trade ended in 1985, when nos 88–90 were extensively refurbished as part of the Park Mall shopping centre development. (*Bryan Sales*)

Upper High Street, 1966. A splendid view illustrating two of Ashford's lost trades of the past. Knowles & Co. (Ashford) Ltd, house furnishers and removal contractors, at no. 106; and the memorable James & Kither, milliners and costumiers, at no. 104. Today Toni & Guy, hairdresser, occupy no. 106 and mobile telephone providers T-Mobile occupy no. 104. (*Bryan Sales*)

The Upper High Street junction with Castle Street, 1966. Further to the left, the Castle Hotel is seen standing prominently at the junction of Castle Street, High Street and New Rents. To the dismay of regulars, the Castle closed in 1997 and became new premises for the Halifax. Upon its closure it had clocked up over 100 years as a licensed premises, and was originally known as the Kings Head prior to 1862. The formidable Crameri's Restaurant stood on the opposite corner, locals still mourning its loss almost forty years after its closure. Crameri's later became Record Corner in the 1970s, and was the home of Our Price records throughout the 1980s. Today nos 108–10 are the home of Phones 4 U. Mobile telephone outlets in the town seem to be an almighty trend nowadays, with so many networks to choose from, for a device not even thought of when this picture was taken. (*Bryan Sales*)

Upper High Street, 1966. A magnificent display of costume in this superb view of Marcus Army and Navy Stores at 100 High Street. At one time the premises of Hugh Penfold, photographer, Marcus' was renowned for their extensive range of leisure wear, equipment and army surplus range. They amalgamated with Millets of St Albans, who were also in the town and still survive in Park Mall. Almost full circle, no. 100 was again to become the home to a photography business when the popular Snappy Snaps opened in 2004. (*Bryan Sales*)

Middle Row, 1966. A nostalgic look at one of the most photographed sites in town. The Man of Kent pub can be seen to the left, together with the premises of A.R. Doughty, tobacconist, at no. 2, which also had shops in Bank Street and New Rents during this time. The popular Marjorie Smith, needlework and wool shop, can be seen to the extreme right adjacent to the pram. It is interesting to note the absence of the Saracens Head Hotel, which is quite clear and apparent when looking beyond the pram towards North Street. A hoarding has been erected while Ashford's first self-service Sainsbury's is being built. Upon its opening, its design was deemed to be state-of-the-art and ahead of its time. (*Bryan Sales*)

The Bank Street junction with Middle Street, 1966. This handsome building, still a familiar landmark in the town, was for many years Swinards World Travel, but back at the time of this picture no. 26 was the premise of Northern Assurance Co. Ltd. Swinards did have a shop next door, but they were then known as Swinards Luxury Coaches Ltd. Ashford Beauty Salon and the Co-op Bakers and confectioners just creep into the extreme right of the picture at no. 24. Latterly the Co-op Chemist, Lloyds Pharmacy, now operates from no. 24. Many will recognise some of the advertising slogans of the time, which include Ovaltine: 'Helps put back what the day takes out!', and bottled Guinness: 'Plan ... Elevation'. It is rare nowadays to find adverts attached to town-centre buildings, and it is not encouraged by the local authority. (*Bryan Sales*)

Bank Street, 1966. One of a number of tobacconists in the town at this time, the premises of A.R Doughty at 37 Bank Street is seen here with Hardies, greeting cards and stationers (previously W. Thompson), at no. 35b. Doughty's also had premises at 2 Middle Row and 4 New Rents, the latter being taken over by A.C. and M.F.E. Maple. The offices of Alfred J. Burrows & Co. can be seen to the right at nos 39–41, which was rebuilt in the late 1990s to become the ever-popular Utopia Bar and Restaurant. The work involved gutting the interior of the old estate agents and retaining the fascia. A new extension was built at the rear, in sympathetic keeping with the original building's design. (*Bryan Sales*)

Middle Street, 1966. Difficult to remember today, Ashford Motors are seen here in their prime at Middle Street. Their garage was demolished in 1972 to make way for a service yard, and today there is no trace of them ever being there. Next door, T. Headley, builders and decorators, and also Kent Sweet Works, wholesale confectioner, were also to fall foul of the bulldozers. Perhaps someone can shed some light on an old rumour that female pump attendants could be seen filling cars with fuel in bikinis in summertime. Bring back the sixties, that's what I say! (*Bryan Sales*)

Middle Street, 1966. Another nostalgic view of Ashford Motors, this time looking towards Bank Street. Chas Boddy, fabrics, and Irene, ladies' hairdresser, can be seen in the background. (*Bryan Sales*)

Bank Street, December 1966. A busy shopping day is captured in this view of Bank Street, taken from outside no. 29, which was the premises of Co-op Funeral Directors for a number of years. Work is currently underway to remodel the road and paving in Bank Street using block work and granite stone, and was due to be completed in October 2008. (*Bryan Sales*)

Bank Street, December 1966. This view illustrates several of the popular traders in the street back in the 1960s. On the extreme left, national shoe chain Freeman, Hardy & Willis Ltd, shoe and boot retailer, once occupied no. 21, while scores of housewives will remember Mence Smith, groceries and hardware, at no. 23. Also illustrated are the Ashford Institute at Whitfeld Hall, with Irene ladies' hairdresser below at no. 25a; Chas Boddy, fabrics, at no. 25b; Mackeson and Co. Ltd, beer, wine and spirit merchant, at no. 27; and also V. Budge, leather goods, at no. 27a. The Co-op Funeral Directors are seen on the extreme right of the picture at no. 29. Few of these familiar names are still trading today. (*Bryan Sales*)

New Street, 1966. This trio of once-thriving businesses in the town are guaranteed to open the floodgates of Ashford as we once knew it. Scores of sixties children and teenagers will remember E. Collins, Tank Milk Bar, which was directly opposite the Tank at nos 3–5 New Street, and was very much a key meeting point for the youngsters of that decade, until its demise in the late 1970s. Reputable estate agent, Daniels, are seen here with their auction rooms at no. 7, and operated there until the early 1970s. For many years, Gouldens Wools and Fancy Goods to the right occupied no. 9, supplying decades of knitters – they too disappeared many years back. (*Bryan Sales*)

New Street, 1966. Well-known local businessman Sonny Hanson was not only known for his connections with motor racing and films of the town, but also his fried fish restaurant in New Street at its junction with Gilbert Road. Many will remember the familiar painting of a 'chef' adorning the upper storey of his premises, and his quality standards in Britain's most famous and probably favourite meal. He was later succeeded by his nephew, Bill Saltmarsh, but sadly the business closed in the early 1980s. No. 15 is now the home of the splendid furniture store, Bakudi. The top of New Street can be seen in the distance to the left. (*Bryan Sales*)

New Street, 1966. Another rare view showing Ashford Car Hire and the premises of Edward 'Skip' Hudson, cycle agent, at nos 27–9. Ashford Car Hire was particularly well known for their providing of wedding cars. It is interesting to note the advertising posters on the side of the building. For instance, films showing at the cinema at the time were *Tarzan and the Valley of Gold* and *Battle of the Bulge*, starring Henry Fonda and Robert Shaw. Today the ring road at Forge Lane passes through where nos 27–9 once stood. (*Bryan Sales*)

New Street, 1966. The vacant premises of Briscall Studios, signwriter and silk screen printer, at no. 73, after they had moved to more modern premises in the town. Owned by true gentleman and well-known Ashford historian Walter Briscall, the business had at one time been located in Norwood Street. Walter was said to have painted the 'cottage' painting that still adorns the walls today, that of the former Olde Cottage Restaurant in North Street, and was reputed to have been furious that the painting had been 'botched' to accommodate the new business names of a short succession of new owners. Sadly Walter is no longer with us, but his work in local history circles still goes on, as he was involved in the establishment of Ashford Museum. The former studios were later demolished for the ring road construction. (*Bryan Sales*)

New Street, 1966. This exceptional view depicts yet another of the town's past trades. Earl & Co. (Ashford) Ltd, second-hand car dealers, at nos 79–81, are seen here with their selection of now classic cars. They were situated opposite Hayward's Garage, which were taken over by Caffyn's in 1967, and upon the alterations to New Street were also demolished in 1972. Incidentally, much of New Street was 'Compulsorily Purchased' at this time. (*Bryan Sales*)

New Street, 1966. In the years before the advent of the wide range of national chains that we today rely on, there were many more small shops in the town. One of three in New Street for many years was The Little Shop, tobacconist and confectioner, next door to Earl's, also at nos 79–81. Complete with its bubble gum and sweet machines outside, it was typical of how those 'little shops' looked in days gone by. Cigarette advertising was also particularly big in the sixties, something that is illegal in modern times owing to the countless numbers of deaths from smoking. The other two stores in the street at the time were Leavers at no. 127, and Violet Perkins, next door to the British Volunteer public house at no. 50. (*Bryan Sales*)

New Street/Maidstone Road, 1966. Clearly showing the absence of St John Ambulance headquarters, Furley Hall, this view shows the former St Teresa's R.C. school, adjacent to the original Church of St Teresa of Avila, designed by Edward Pugin. The school later moved to new, purpose-built premises in Quantock Drive, and the church illustrated was demolished in the 1990s to be replaced by a new church of modern design. The house that once formed part of the school is now privately owned. (*Bryan Sales*)

New Street/Barrow Hill, 1966. No longer standing today, this view shows the junction of Barrow Hill and New Street alongside the Prince of Orange, and nos 113–17 prior to their demolition for the Magazine Road roundabout. (*Bryan Sales*)

New Street, 1966. One of the town's well-known tobacconists, Leavers is seen here in this excellent view at no. 127. Owned by kindly gentleman Mr C.J. Leaver, locals will remember the other premises owned by him in the town at 6 Bank Street and 1b Middle Row, the latter still trading today as Leavers, with Mr Leaver's daughter-in-law, Anne, still working there. The interior of the Middle Row premises has remained much the same as it did over forty years ago, providing a 'time-capsule-like' look at Ashford's past. (*Bryan Sales*)

Magazine Road, 1966. The two quaint cottages illustrated here, nos 2 and 4, were adjacent to E.K. Chittenden's joinery works, and were demolished in 1974 for the Magazine Road roundabout. (*Bryan Sales*)

New Rents, 1966. This fascinating period view shows New Rents at its junction with Hempsted Street. Well-known bakers and confectioners Nicholas Kingsman can be seen on the left at nos 1–5, with the yard entrance of the Castle Hotel on the right. A sign of the times, note the adverts on the wall next to the Central Pie shop. One of the adverts states that you could rent a 15in television from Radio Rentals for 6/6, roughly 41 new pence, a week. (*Bryan Sales*)

North Street junction with Middle Row, 1966. This ancient part of the town has been much photographed over the decades. On closer inspection, it shows the memorable Bartlett and Best, saddlers, at no. 2a. Mr Best is reputed to have been based mainly down in the basement of the premises, and if his shop assistant required assistance he would call down 'Mr Best, Sir! Mr Best, Sir!' The familiar premises of Doughty, tobacconist, at no. 2 can be seen adjacent to the passage through to the church. The formidable Mocha Bar, owned by A. and T.A. Rossi, can be seen on the extreme left, and Skinners (of Faversham) Ltd, radio, television and gramophone suppliers, can be seen on the extreme right. (*Bryan Sales*)

Lower High Street, 1966. A splendid view showing J. Ingall & Son, chemists, at no. 42, with Keith R.A. Skinner, opticians, above at no. 42a, which were previously the premises of Salon Margaret, owned by Margaret Whitling. Photocraft (Kent) Ltd at no. 40 was run by reputable businessman Victor Matthews, who latterly established Studio Photocraft at 15 High Street. Nowadays known as Soundcraft Hi-fi, Victor's son, Geoff, continues to specialise in top-quality audio and visual equipment, having parted company with the photography side several years ago. Consort Specialized publicity service and E. Beasley, dyers and cleaners, can be seen to the right at no. 38. (*Bryan Sales*)

Lower High Street, December 1966. In the years before the likes of Next, River Island and Debenhams, Sercombe's were a 'must' in the choice of clothing retailer in the town. Their men's and children's shop, illustrated here at no. 1a, was renowned for its quality for over thirty years in the town. They also had a Jaeger-branded ladies' outfitters at no. 12. It was not until the 1980s when their focus was directed just to menswear from their shop at 30 North Street. Sadly, the Sercombe's name disappeared in the early 1990s after the untimely death of the then proprietor. (*Bryan Sales*)

Lower High Street, December 1966. An exceptional view of no. 31 High Street, known locally as St John's Chambers. Once known as a public house with the unusual name of The Ounce's Head, no. 31 is today known as Halifax Estate Agents. Back in 1966, the premises was split into three. For many years the left of the premises was Victoria Wine Co., the centre of no. 31 was Betabake Bakeries, and to the right, together with the upper floors, was reputable estate agent and chartered surveyor, Scott Kendon and Ronald Pearce. (*Bryan Sales*)

Lower High Street, December 1966. This memorable view shows the once-familiar Globe Art Wallpapers Ltd at no. 21, now commonly known as Antoniou Hairdressers. Next door, the popular Bon Bon Snack Bar at no. 23, owned by the well-respected Matassa family, later became a kebab shop in the 1990s. The Westbourne Park Building Society at no. 25, on the right, is today a dance and schoolwear shop. (*Bryan Sales*)

Lower High Street, December 1966. A fantastic view showing some of our lost shop fronts of the 1960s. One of the town's oldest grocers, Headley, can be seen on the left at no. 46, with the printer side of the family's shop at no. 44. Next we see J. Ingall & Son, chemist, at no. 42 and Photocraft (Kent) Ltd, photographic dealers, at no. 40, owned by well-known figure and respected businessman Victor Matthews. (*Bryan Sales*)

Lower High Street, December 1966. Further to the right and down the High Street, this view shows E. Beasley and Son Ltd, dyers and cleaners, at no. 38; B.J. Marsh, the seedsman, at no. 36; and Ashford Co-operative Society's Tobacconist just creeping into view on the right at no. 34. (*Bryan Sales*)

Lower High Street, December 1966. Sandwiched between Marshall's Gowns at no. 16 and Halford Cycle Co. Ltd, cycle and motor accessories, at no. 12, the popular ladies' and gents' hairdresser The Ideal is seen here, with their 'rogues gallery' of hairstyles from the sixties, at no. 14. Although no longer situated here, forty-three years later they haven't moved far. Still proving popular, and still snipping hundreds of heads, they are trading above no. 14 to this day. (*Bryan Sales*)

Lower High Street, December 1966. For many years no. 5 was known as The Royal Oak public house, but is better recognised as Alfred Olby Ltd, builders merchants and ironmongers, as illustrated in this view. Olby's also had premises at the corner of High Street and Station Road at no. 1, housing their wallpaper and paint department. Sadly, upon the advent of large chains such as B&Q and Homebase, Olby's closed in 1968 after a number of years supplying those do-it-yourself enthusiasts in the town. No. 5, together with its adjoining premises at nos 1 and 3, were demolished the same year for redevelopment, replacing these former landmarks with Pearl Assurance House. (*Bryan Sales*)

Lower High Street, December 1966. Not instantly memorable, this view shows no. 3 when occupied by Bazaar, costumiers and milliners, another of the town's architectural gems that was sacrificed at the end of the 1960s. (*Bryan Sales*)

2

PAST TIMES

Bank Street, 1962. This and the following fantastic views were commissioned by Ashford Urban District Council in 1962, and were originally taken mainly in portrait fashion, in order for them to join together. In the days before computer wizardry, this was near impossible, but they hold so much detail of Ashford's quaint past that they are shown here in their individual frames with a few exceptions, bearing in mind the age of the negatives. This first view portrays Bank Street at its junction with Godinton Road, looking towards the High Street. (*Studio Photocraft/David Worsley*)

Bank Street junction with Godinton Road, 1962. A fascinating view of an undisturbed Godinton Road, in the days before the vast redevelopment in this part of the town. Beer lovers will remember the Market Hotel, latterly renamed the Wig and Gavel in the 1970s, which has disappeared in recent years. Wright Brothers, sports outfitters, at no. 38 can be seen on the right-hand corner, for many years run by Mr Keston-Hole. Many of the distant properties both on the left and right of the street were demolished in large sections as early as 1970, and the first stages of the ring road in 1971 severed Godinton Road for good. The new County Square extension today leaves this once largely residential area totally unrecognisable. (*Studio Photocraft/David Worsley*)

Bank Street, 1962. Here we see Wright Brothers' familiar shop front at its Bank Street elevation. Oxfam occupied no. 38 for many years after Wrights closed, and today the corner property is popular gaming centre Olympia Leisure. (*Studio Photocraft/David Worsley*)

Bank Street, 1962. Still trading in Folkestone, Newman's furnishers once occupied no. 36. Renowned for second-hand furnishings in East Kent, at the time they also had a shop in Hythe, which has since closed. Popular flooring specialist Philip Clark and Ski and Street, skiwear, occupied no. 38 during the late 1970s and early 1980s. Today Perfect Pizza runs their popular business from the premises. Just creeping into the picture, no. 34 is occupied by P. Hawksfield & Son, coal and coke merchants, who were later succeeded by Corralls. Today the property is split – Nasrin Indian Takeaway occupies the left, while a nail studio occupies the right. (*Studio Photocraft/David Worsley*)

Bank Street, 1962. Reputable auctioneer and estate agent, W. & B. Hobbs, had for many years been a key player in the property market in the town. In subsequent years the name change to Hobbs Parker, and their later residential property department in North Street was taken over by Cornerstone/Abbey National in the 1990s. Still a success today, Hobbs Parker excels in all property areas and reintroduced their residential department when a move was made to the new Ashford market. Locals will remember their premises at 32 Bank Street, illustrated here. (*Studio Photocraft/David Worsley*)

Bank Street, 1962. A superb view showing Martin Watts, ladies' hairdresser, and W. Giles & Son, glass and china merchants, at nos 30 and 30a. Giles & Son were a formidable name in this trade for over forty years in the town, and there has not been a competitor matching this accolade since its closure in the early 1970s. In the 1980s Corkers Wine Bar proved popular as a nightspot with local people, and then in recent years with Bransky's Brasserie during daytime trade. In 2001, in a bid to revive a past trend, Corkers was reborn, but this was short lived, and thriving bar and restaurant Threezero opened, providing a touch of class and art deco in the town. (*Studio Photocraft/ David Worsley*)

Bank Street, 1962. For many years no. 28 has been home to Shelter, a charity shop, but back in 1962 the familiar building was home to the South Eastern Gas showrooms. Clearly dating this picture, an advert in the window suggests 'Isn't it time you had a 1962 cooker!' There are probably still people in the town with a 1962 model – things were built to last in those days. The gas showrooms later moved into the Tufton Centre in 1975. (*Studio Photocraft/ David Worsley*)

Bank Street, 1962. A rare view showing one of the beehive-styled porches that were once part of the Methodist Church. Sinfully, the local council passed planning permission to remove these original features in 1969, in order to build The Centrepiece rooms and youth club. The result – two unsightly 1960s-style brick wings, which are one-dimensional and out of keeping with the church's original design. In 2003, plans were put forward to replace these eyesores with futuristic glass replacements, but owing to a lack of funding, plans have yet to come to fruition. (*Studio Photocraft/David Worsley*)

Bank Street, 1962. The Methodist Church, in its original state, prior to the alterations of the late 1960s. The gates and boundary wall have long gone and a series of steps to the pavement are a more familiar sight. (*Studio Photocraft/David Worsley*)

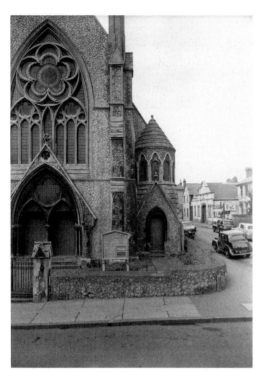

Bank Street, 1962. This photograph shows the right-hand beehive-styled porch with Middle Street on the extreme right. The minister at the time was the Revd John V. Wilson. (*Studio Photocraft/David Worsley*)

Bank Street junction with Middle Street, 1962. Not instantly recognisable today, this view shows Middle Street prior to its severance for the Tufton Centre. Hempsted Street can be seen in the background. Reputable garage Ashford Motors can be seen (centre right) together with the Kent Sweet Works, wholesale confectioners, along towards the Hempsted Street junction. Today the street is much altered, providing service access to the rear of lower Bank Street premises and much of the south end of County Square Shopping Centre. (*Studio Photocraft/ David Worsley*)

Bank Street, 1962. A fantastic period view showing one of several Co-op outlets in the town at the time. Their bakery and confectionery premises at no. 24 can be seen here in all its splendour. The popular Ashford Beauty Salon above the Co-op once proved a hit with those glamour girls of the sixties, being particularly well known for their ladies' hairdressing. The confectionery and bakery latterly became the Co-op chemists in the early 1970s, after they moved from 102 High Street, and the salon disappeared during this transition. Lloyds Pharmacy now operates from no. 24. (*Studio Photocraft/David Worsley*)

Bank Street, 1962. Burnage's were renowned for their quality for a number of years in the town. Previously located in the High Street where Woolworth's stood before it closed in early 2009, Burnage's specialised in pianoforte, radio, television and household appliances from their handsome premises at no. 22, once owned by the Brabourne family. Much sadness was felt from Burnage's regular clients when the traditional shop closed in 1983, notching up over seventy-five years in the town. Kent material firm Cross's now occupy no. 22, providing everything for the artist, including stationery, printing and quality and friendly service. (*Studio Photocraft/ David Worsley*)

Bank Street, 1962. The wonderfully ornate doorway of no. 22 is clearly illustrated here. At the time of this photograph the offices of the Probation Service were located above Burnage's. (*Studio Photocraft/David Worsley*)

Bank Street, 1962. Well-known gentlemen's outfitter Frank Manning can be seen here at no. 20, a business which only disappeared as recently as 1980. In recent years the premises have been Bransky's bakery and an art gallery, but nowadays no. 20 is the ever-popular Ashford Café, owned by successful local businessman Ufuk Shen, who also owns Barry's Kitchen, Cornerstone Bed and Breakfast and Café Express. (*Studio Photocraft/David Worsley*)

Bank Street, 1962. An image rarely found in individual collections, this superb view shows the locally renowned Mac Fisheries, fish merchants and poulterers, at no. 18a. Many Ashfordians still reminisce about Mac Fisheries and the neighbouring trade of W. Trice, greengrocer and fruiterer, at no. 18, who latterly had a florist's shop at the same premises for many years. The reputable greengrocer and fruiterer also had premises at 4 Middle Row, which had previously been Barkers, high-class fruiterers, and Waghorne butchers. (*Studio Photocraft/David Worsley*)

Bank Street junction with Tufton Street (east), 1962. A splendid and nostalgic view depicting Tufton Street in the days prior to its severance for the Tufton Centre, changing the face of this central quarter of the town forever. The established Elwick Club can be seen on the right, adjacent to the central Post Office (centre right). Panorama Rentals, radio and television, can be seen on the left at no. 20, adjacent to Flynn's the Cleaner at no. 22, the latter becoming a Wimpy Bar in 1977. Many residents will remember the two hostelries sacrificed for the Tufton Centre, namely the Wellington Hotel and the Coach and Horses, which can be identified clearly in the distance at the junction of Hempsted Street. (*Studio Photocraft/David Worsley*)

Bank Street, 1962. A magnificent and atmospheric view of Bank Street in its pre-development days, and when upkeep and appearance of both property and street were deemed to be of importance. The basic structure of the street remains today, but the atmosphere of days gone by has long since faded into history. Efforts are currently being undertaken to reclaim and revive the street as a key location for shopping and business in the town. (*Studio Photocraft/David Worsley*)

Tufton Street, 1962. Another view of Tufton Street (east), showing nos 20–36. Incidentally, nos 28–36 alone were demolished for the Tufton Centre. (*Studio Photocraft/David Worsley*)

Bank Street, 1962. Here we see a splendid view showing the upper section of Bank Street in 1962. (*Studio Photocraft/David Worsley*)

Bank Street, 1962. This is another fascinating view showing one of the many bakers and pastry cooks in the town during the 1960s. Nicholas Kingsman the baker, illustrated here at no. 16, had another popular shop in the town at 1–5 New Rents. Both will be remembered for their gorgeous cakes and pastries. It is a different story in the town over forty years later. Businesses of individual trade such as butchers, bakers and pastry cooks, are such a rarity nowadays, probably owing to the advent of chain stores throughout the last thirty years. This prime Bank Street premises had at one time been Lipton's Tea Co. and in the 1970s a ladies' fashion store by the name of Jean Jeannie. (*Studio Photocraft/David Worsley*)

Bank Street, 1962. Although many people have fond memories of the 1960s, times could be hard and the essentials in life were sometimes difficult to come by. For instance, many people could not afford a television set. Multi Broadcast, illustrated here at no. 14, enabled those in need to rent a set, whereas today there has been a steep decline in the need to rent, with the price of new and owned equipment becoming cheaper and cheaper. (*Studio Photocraft/David Worsley*)

Bank Street, 1962. Gizzi's Café, illustrated here at no. 12, will be remembered by many Ashfordians for their high standards and immaculate restaurants in the town. Owners Vilma and Antonio Gizzi will always be remembered, in particular for their large restaurant at no. 29 High Street, of which they retired from in the early 1990s. Gizzi's originally came to the town in the early 1960s and at one time had reputable businesses in East Sussex. (*Studio Photocraft/David Worsley*)

Bank Street, 1962. A splendid period view of one of the many butchers in the town in past times. C. Kingston Ltd, butchers, are seen here at no. 10, which latterly became Burrows and Co. estate agent, in addition to their offices at 39–41 Bank Street. In recent years no. 10 became a popular jeanswear store, Just Jeans, run by admired businessman Lloyd Woodward and his faithful assistant, Juanita Sobhee.
(*Studio Photocraft/David Worsley*)

Bank Street, 1962. Generations of knitters will remember the tiny wool shop, run for many years by Mrs M.L. Evernden at no. 10a. The business continued well into the 1970s, and no. 10a later became the offices for the local newspaper, the *Ashford Citizen*. On closer inspection nos 10 and 10a were previously one shop, and for many years were occupied by a china shop, with no. 10a retaining part of the original shop front as seen today. (*Studio Photocraft/David Worsley*)

Bank Street, 1962. Here we see the once-familiar premises of E. Strange, drapers and milliners, at no. 8, who were trading in the town until the 1990s and then at later premises at 52 High Street. Strange's were renowned for their 'Aladdin's cave' atmosphere. In recent years the business was owned by Brian Strange and then it was sold to Wards', who continue to carry on the reputable trade that Strange's laid the foundation for. No. 8 has more recently been the home of the Woolwich Building Society, now part of Barclays. (*Studio Photocraft/ David Worsley*)

Bank Street, 1962. This particularly rare view shows Seamores, confectioners and tobacconist, latterly Leaver's, at no. 6 with Penny's Snack Bar, also at no. 6. Upon its closure, the tobacconist became well-known estate agency Butler and Hatch Waterman, and in 1999 became part of the Woolwich, while Penny's Snack Bar became the popular restaurant Barry's Kitchen in 1979, originally selling delicatessen meats and pastries.
(*Studio Photocraft/David Worsley*)

Bank Street, 1962. In the days before the larger chain additions to the town, it had much more individuality than today. Here we see the premises of C.J. Stapley, chemists, at no. 4. Other well-remembered chemists in the town at the time were F. Gutteridge's at 107 High Street and J. Ingall & Son at no. 42. Both of these are no longer trading today, owing to the advent of the larger companies such as Boots, Lloyd's and Paydens. Stapley's later became G'Day Sport in the 1980s and is now the home of Demelza House, a charity shop. (*Studio Photocraft/ David Worsley*)

Bank Street, 1962. Not instantly recognisable today, this view shows no. 2d, Phillips Bros (Character Shoes), prior to nos 2c and 2 (right) being demolished in 1972 to create a service area for the Tufton Centre. Today, with the absence of this highly decorative building, it leaves an unsightly gap. In 2004, plans were afoot to replace this architectural gem with a building of similar design and incorporating an archway, but these plans have yet to come to fruition. The shoe shop later became an off-licence, a mobile telephone outlet and, in early 2000, Buzz men's hairdressers. (*Studio Photocraft/David Worsley*)

Bank Street, 1962. Although not showing the beautiful building at its best, this view shows Andrews shoe shop at no. 2c and Cyco Rado Ltd, cycles, radios and electrical agents, at no. 2. Still reputable today, Geering & Colyer, estate agent (now opposite), once had offices above these shops. (*Studio Photocraft/ David Worsley*)

Bank Street, 1962. An unusual view showing nos 2–2c where it adjoins National Provincial Bank at no. 2a. Who is that person posing in the photograph? (*Studio Photocraft/David Worsley*)

Bank Street, 1962. In answer to the previous question, this side of Bank Street couldn't be tied up without including this close-up of Studio Photocraft's young apprentice David Worsley. David went on to be a recognised professional photographer, and back in the 1960s worked with such respected photographers as Victor Matthews, Arthur Rust and Jack Adam of Hythe. (*Studio Photocraft/David Worsley*)

Bank Street, 1962. A magnificent view showing National Provincial Bank at no. 2a, which at the time was also the offices of the Ministry of Fuel and Power, District Inspector of Quarries and Mines and J.A. Conrad, L.R.I.B.A, chartered architect. The bank was later merged with National Westminster Bank and in 1994 became Stoodley Phippen, solicitors, subsequently merging with reputable Kent solicitor Girlings, who also have premises in Canterbury and Margate. (*Studio Photocraft/ David Worsley*)

Bank Street, 1962. This nostalgic look shows the east side of Bank Street, in the days before the street was largely pedestrianised. Here we see Hepworth's men's outfitter at the corner of Bank Street and the High Street in its prominent position. Many years ago, this was the premises of well-known Ashford photographer Alaric Hawkins De'Ath, but today 83 High Street is more familiarly known as the premises of Thomson travel agents, part of the TUI group. (*Studio Photocraft/ David Worsley*)

Bank Street, 1962. The handsome premises of Lloyds Bank Limited (latterly Lloyds TSB) can be seen here dominating Bank Street at its junction with High Street. This was the site of the original Ashford Bank which was established by the Jemmett family, although the building has been extensively rebuilt and remodelled. Many locals will remember the zebra crossing which stood at the top of Bank Street and later disappeared in the early 1970s, although this part of the street was not traffic-free until 1989. (*Studio Photocraft/ David Worsley*)

Bank Street junction with High Street, 1962. Here we see the familiar entrance still used today at Lloyds Bank Ltd in Kings Parade. Middle Row can be seen in the background to the left. (*Studio Photocraft/David Worsley*)

Bank Street, 1962. This view shows the side elevation as seen from Bank Street in the days when glass panels of banks were sign-written. One of the services offered in 1962 was 'Foreign Business Transacted' as illustrated on one of the windows. Services offered today have come on tremendously from what they were in the 1960s. Lloyds continue to offer numerous services tailored to suit the individual needs of the modern client. (*Studio Photocraft/David Worsley*)

Bank Street, 1962. The side entrance to Lloyds Bank, which at the time was the access to the Executor and Trustees department and also the offices of the Liverpool Victoria Friendly Society, which was situated on the upper floors. At one point the upper floors of the bank were individually let for the most unconnected of purposes. For instance there was a dentist's surgery located above the bank at one time. (*Studio Photocraft/David Worsley*)

Bank Street, 1962. Reputable and long-standing auctioneer and land agent, Geering and Colyer, are seen here at Bank Chambers, at one time the garden of the main bank buildings. The archway to the left is the rear access for vehicles to the bank, and is still in use today. The business was once part of Lloyds in their Black Horse division but, upon Lloyd's amalgamation with the Trustee Savings Bank, the property agency was sold to Bradford & Bingley. The commercial department Colyer Commercial, now privately run, still survives at 15 Tufton Street, the former printing works of Thompson, the well-known Ashford Printer and adjacent to the Swan Public house. (*Studio Photocraft/David Worsley*)

Bank Street, 1962. Back in 1962 Geering and Colyer only occupied one side of the ground floor of Bank Chambers. The central entrance, seen here, led to their upper-floor offices. The chambers were once the registered offices of Lamberts Crushed Beach Ltd and Cobbs Wood Development (Ashford) Ltd. Still a key figure in the property world, Geering and Colyer today occupy the whole of the Bank Chambers.
(*Studio Photocraft/David Worsley*)

Bank Street, 1962. Although part of the Bank Chambers, Newton Hadfield, dyers and cleaners, were once situated at 1 Bank Street. There were many more cleaners in the town during the 1960s and '70s, including 3 Day Cleaners in Park Road, Kengate Beasley in the High Street and Tufton Street, Flynns in Tufton Street and Middle Row and Advance Laundry in Kings Parade. Up until recently, there was only one. One must remember that not everybody could afford a washing machine back then. (*Studio Photocraft/ David Worsley*)

Bank Street, 1962. Another of the long-term banking institutions in the town is Barclays Bank, seen here at 3 Bank Street. Of course, the name of the street has no bearing on the type of business situated there. Barclays later moved to the lower High Street at no. 13 before moving again to larger premises at 64–6 High Street, (formerly Marks and Spencer) in 1979. After an absence of over thirty years and upon the amalgamation of the Woolwich with Barclays, they once more have premises opposite their original premises of no. 3, at nos 6–8, formerly the Woolwich and Butler and Hatch Waterman, estate agent. They retain their High Street premises and business centre in North Street. (*Studio Photocraft/David Worsley*)

Bank Street, 1962. A fantastic view showing the now rather dated shop front of Victor's costumiers and milliners at no. 5, which was situated in the town for a number of years. Upon the demise of Victor's in the late 1970s, no. 5 became the Halifax Building Society until 1997, when they moved to the former Castle Inn at 1 Castle Street. Prior to the construction of Pearl Assurance House at the foot of the High Street, their offices were located above Victor's, at one time occupied by Thompson the printer. It is interesting to note that, on inspecting the door to the immediate left, although over painted, the name 'THOMPSON' can still be seen today on the letter box, which at one time would have been polished brass. (*Studio Photocraft/ David Worsley*)

Bank Street, 1962. The familiar premises of reputable solicitors Kingsford, Flower and Pain are seen here at no. 7, in the days prior to their expansion. Established in the early nineteenth century by Julius Kingsford, the firm are renowned locally for their professional services. In 1997 the names of one-time partners 'Flower' and 'Pain' were dropped in favour of a more modern approach. During that time, they also expanded into the former premises of the Halifax at no. 5, and the entrance illustrated was blocked to allow a new reception to be made re-using the former Halifax shop front. Today Kingsford's continue to excel in the world of law and property. (*Studio Photocraft/David Worsley*)

Bank Street, 1962. The vacant premises of no. 8 which had previously been the offices of the Royal Insurance Company, and, before that, those of Curry Cycle Co. Shortly after this photograph was taken, the premises became part of Hallett & Co. Solicitors, situated to the right of the picture. (*Studio Photocraft/David Worsley*)

Bank Street, 1962. Another established law firm in the town, Hallett & Co., are seen here at nos 9–13, nowadays situated next door to Kingsford's, but at the time of this picture it was separated by the former premises of Royal Insurance Company. Originally known as Hallett, Creery, Welldon and Creery, the firm became Hallett & Co. from 1830, and had premises at 11 Bank Street. At one time Hallett's had other locations in the town – in New Rents in 1831 and in North Street in 1887. The firm specialises in Commissioning for Oaths and Notaries Public. (*Studio Photocraft/ David Worsley*)

Bank Street, 1962. Another view showing the familiar premises of Hallett & Co. (*Studio Photocraft/David Worsley*)

Bank Street, 1962. Once located at the junction of Bank Street and Tufton Street, here we see the familiar premises of G. Herbert & Co. Ltd, pawnbrokers, jewellers, outfitters and furniture dealers, at no. 15. The established business was located at this prime corner in the town for over thirty years, and will be fondly remembered by locals. The business disappeared in 1971 and the premises were split. The elevation illustrated later became the Turntable Record Shop around the same time. The other half of the premises became G. Edbrooke, gentlemen's outfitter, which stretched around into Tufton Street and for many years had been at 31 High Street. None of the names mentioned are still in business today. (*Studio Photocraft/David Worsley*)

Bank Street junction with Tufton Street, 1962. Another view showing the corner elevation of the familiar pawnbrokers business. Note the trademark hanging pawnbrokers balls on the upper elevation. (*Studio Photocraft/David Worsley*)

Bank Street junction with Tufton Street, 1962. This is a splendid view of Tufton Street, looking towards Church Road and Vicarage Lane. The Swan Hotel can be seen further down on the left, and the Royal Insurance Company at 17 Bank Street can be seen on the right. Note the absence of the old Picture Palace on the right adjacent to the lamp post, which had been demolished shortly before this picture was taken. (*Studio Photocraft/David Worsley*)

Bank Street, 1962. A magnificent view showing the upper (Westside) of Bank Street at its best, back in a gentler and calmer era. (*Studio Photocraft/David Worsley*)

Bank Street, 1962. This wonderful view shows a deserted lower Bank Street at its junction with Tufton Street. The street is still instantly recognisable today, but the traffic flow is now one-way in the direction of the High Street. It is probable that this view may well have been taken on a Sunday. For the past twenty or so years, Bank Street has mainly been dominated by buses. (*Studio Photocraft/David Worsley*)

Bank Street, 1962. Still recognisable today, despite the addition of a modern shop front, here we see the premises of the Royal Insurance Company at no. 17, who were also agents for the Liverpool, London & Globe Insurance Co. Ltd. The reputable national insurer remained in these premises until the late 1980s. The lower sash-style windows were removed and replaced with a modern-style shop front upon the acquisition of no. 17 by the Cheltenham & Gloucester, who still occupy the premises today.
(*Studio Photocraft/David Worsley*)

Bank Street, 1962. In the absence of yellow lines, a lone Vespa motorcycle stands outside the premises. Today, parking is a totally different case, with strict parking regulations throughout the town centre. On an embarrassing note, a 'rookie' parking attendant employed by the local authority recently posted a ticket on a hearse outside F.C. Wood's funeral directors in Tufton Street. If a bonus scheme was in place, I don't think one was earned for this mishap. (*Studio Photocraft/ David Worsley*)

Bank Street, 1962. Long before the days of any merger on the cards, the Trustee Savings Bank is seen in its original location in the town at no. 19. More recently known as just T.S.B., they subsequently moved into the former premises of Co-op Funeral Directors and Douglas Weaver's camera shop at nos 29 and 29a respectively. No. 19 ended its time as a bank when the later occupant, Alliance & Leicester, gave way to a new Subway takeaway, which can be found all over the world. Subway is renowned for its fresh and delicious baguettes and sandwiches, and experience an enormous trade at lunchtimes. (*Studio Photocraft/David Worsley*)

Bank Street, 1962. For over forty years Freeman, Hardy & Willis Ltd were a substantial name in the world of shoes and footwear, not just in Ashford but all over the United Kingdom. They are seen here at no. 21, which was also once the premises of Foster Finn-Kelcey & Co., chartered accountant, who occupied the upper floor. The popular shoe shop later moved to 58 High Street, which had previously been the Kent grocer, Vye and Son Ltd. Sadly, the Freeman, Hardy & Willis name seems to be another trusted trade name of the past. (*Studio Photocraft/David Worsley*)

Bank Street, 1962. Many of the older generation, either born Ashfordians or newcomers back in the 1960s, still talk fondly of Mence Smith Ltd, grocery and hardware, at no. 23 – one of a number of traders in the town that are no longer in existence. For the past twenty years, no. 23 has been the home of turf accountant William Hill. The trade is still a popular money-raiser for many. (*Studio Photocraft/ David Worsley*)

Bank Street, 1962. This classic view shows the well-known Whitfeld Hall, built in 1873 at 25 Bank Street. At the time it was occupied by the Ashford Institute, the Toft School of Dancing and Irene ladies' hairdresser, whose proprietor at time was Mrs Irene Sizer. It was not until 1976 that gentlemen's hairdressing was introduced at no. 25a, known as 'Man at Irene'. Today, Cranium Heads still operate a popular hairdressing salon in this once-ornate hall, which has also suffered architecturally from modern alterations. (*Studio Photocraft/David Worsley*)

Bank Street, 1962. Here we see the familiar premises of Chas Boddy fabrics at no. 25a, together with Mackeson & Co. Ltd, beer, wine and spirit merchant, at no. 27. The fabric shop was later taken over by B. & M. Batt of the same trade in the 1970s, and the former off-licence was, for many years, automotive radio specialist Road Radio. Today no. 25a is the premises of an Alternative Chinese Medicine outlet while no. 27 is occupied by long-standing Ashford hairdresser Melvin Brookes with the help of his son, Westleigh. (*Studio Photocraft/David Worsley*)

Bank Street, 1962. Neighbouring Mackeson's, many leather lovers will remember the premises of V. Budge Ltd, leather goods, at no. 27a. The one-time *Adscene Newspaper* office is soon to become *Ashford News*, the first newsagent in Bank Street for over twenty-five years. Further to the right, the Co-operative Funeral Service premises at no. 29 were later remodelled to form the second Trustee Savings Bank premises located in the street. (*Studio Photocraft/David Worsley*)

Bank Street, 1962. Here we see the premises of two of the most respected and memorable photographers of the past in Ashford. Douglas Weaver and his brother, George, were regarded as true professionals in everything photographic between 1949 and 1972, until Douglas sold the business to his one-time apprentice Ian Gambrill and his wife, Sue. The high standards continued and the business was renamed Countrywide Photographic in the late 1970s. George was mainly based in Tenterden, but Douglas operated his photography business at 3 Queen Street together with his Camera Shop at 29a Bank Street, seen here. The late Weaver brothers will always remain in history for their work in the area. (*Studio Photocraft/David Worsley*)

Bank Street, 1962. Although part of a national chain, Curry's are one of the very few businesses of the past that have not only gone from strength to strength but also have changed beyond recognition. Back in the 1950s and '60s, for instance, they also sold bicycles, something they parted with long ago. Today Curry's can rarely be found on the High Street, the company favouring the out-of-town superstores. Upon closer inspection, the advertisements in the window state that you can buy a Triumph bicycle for £24 17s 7d, a Phillips bicycle for £24 10s 2d and a BSA bicycle for £25 17s 5d. A more familiar item of their trade, a transistor radio could be bought in 1962 for £7 19s 6d. (*Studio Photocraft/David Worsley*)

Bank Street, 1962. An exceptional view showing nos 33, 33a and 33b Bank Street, which at the time were occupied by S.V. Semadeni, antiques, second-hand furniture and philatelist, at no. 33; W.A. Oxford, optician, at no. 33a; and A.V. Checksfield, auctioneers, valuers and estate agents, at no. 33b. Today, Linda's Florist occupies the former premises of S.V. Semadeni, while long-term occupant Brownbill's superseded W.A. Oxford in the optician's business. (*Studio Photocraft/David Worsley*)

Bank Street, 1962. This splendid view illustrates the one-time Singer Sewing Centre and W. Thompson, commercial printers and stationers, at nos 35a and 35b, with the offices of Kemp & Kemp, certified accountants, above at no. 35. Singer was commonly known for their worldwide sewing machines, but in this view they are displaying twin-tub washing machines priced at 83 guineas. Other items sold by the well-known manufacturer included typewriters and vacuum cleaners. Long-established printer Thompson's premises later became Hardies Greeting Cards. (*Studio Photocraft/David Worsley*)

Bank Street, 1962. As mentioned earlier, Doughty's tobacconist, seen here at no. 37, will be remembered for their other premises in the town at Middle Row and also New Rents. It is mainly due to the fact that, during the 1970s, large supermarkets introduced kiosks selling cigarettes and confectionery, that supermarkets technically phased out the smaller shops like these in town centres. Despite this, the town still has two, namely the Chocolate Box in the lower High Street and Leaver's in Middle Row – two businesses that have somehow survived to the modern times. (*Studio Photocraft/David Worsley*)

Bank Street, 1962. Although only disappearing within the last twenty-five years, for many newcomers to the town the name Burrows & Co. will mean nothing. However, these one-time reputable estate agents and auctioneers at nos 39–41 were professionals in the property business for over fifty years, along with competitors at the time such as Scott Kendon & Ronald Pearce, and also W.B. Hobbs. The established business later became Burrows & Day in the 1970s and the name changed to Cobbs (inc. Burrows & Day) in the early 1980s. In 1989, during the reign of then owner General Accident, the building was largely redeveloped, which involved the complete demolition of the internal parts of the building, but the familiar classical fascia was retained. General Accident had, by then, moved to Middle Row, and nos 39–41 were extended in the same style as the Bank Street elevation to become Calgarth House. The former offices at street level became popular bar and restaurant Utopia in 1999, creating a new direction for licensed premises in the town, which until then had largely been more public house orientated.
(*Studio Photocraft/David Worsley*)

Bank Street, 1962. Another view showing the familiar Bank Street elevation of nos 39–41.
(*Studio Photocraft/David Worsley*)

Bank Street junction with Queen Street, 1962. This view shows the scrolled stonework above the entrance of Burrows & Co. This 'scroll' is a familiar sight elsewhere in the town – including 83 High Street, which is currently the premises of Thomson Travel, and it can also be seen at 13 New Street, which is currently Seekers Lettings. This style indicates that these three properties were constructed by the same builder. The popular Corn Exchange, which was demolished in 1964, can be seen on the immediate right.
(*Studio Photocraft/David Worsley*)

Bank Street, April 1962. This splendid period view shows the foot of Bank Street where it joins Elwick Road, and at its junction with Godinton Road and Queen Street. (*Studio Photocraft/David Worsley*)

Lower High Street, 1962. This rare view shows the premises of reputable businessman and professional photographer Victor Mathews at 40 High Street. Photocraft (Kent) Ltd and also Studio Photocraft, as they were known, were a trusted name in the town for both equipment and high-quality photography. They occupied numerous locations in the town over the years including 15 and 91 High Street. Here, we see the interior of no. 40 as it looked in 1962, showing its neat displays and staircase to its studio and photographic department. Today no. 40 is the home of Soundcraft Hi-fi which provides professional, high-quality audio-visual equipment. The reputable business is owned by Victor's knowledgeable and gentlemanly son Geoff, with the help of his faithful son, Sam, indicating that in all, father, son and grandson have traded in the town and in particular these premises for over forty years. It was due to a period of general decline in the photography trade that the decision was made to concentrate on the audio-visual side, which necessitated the change of name. (*Studio Photocraft/David Worsley*)

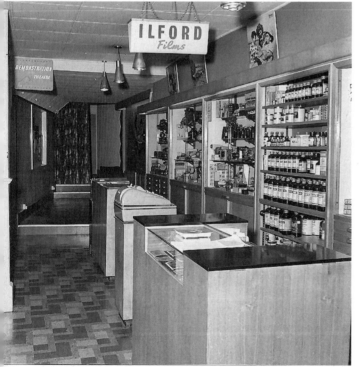

Lower High Street, 1962. Years before the advent of digital photography, domestic darkrooms were extremely popular, and it was an affordable hobby. Rows of darkroom chemicals and equipment can be seen in the cabinets on the right. Further along on the right, both used and new equipment can be seen in plentiful quantities. Like an 'Aladdin's Cave', the popular shop was always well stocked for even the most demanding of photographers. (*Studio Photocraft/David Worsley*)

Lower High Street, 1962. Photocraft also had a tape recorder department next door at no. 38. Here, we see one of Victor's colleagues, Mr Primavasey, talking through the available electronic plugs, jacks and accessories that were available at the time.
(*Studio Photocraft/ David Worsley*)

Lower High Street, 1962. This view illustrates a demonstration by Mr Primavasey of the once-popular reel-to-reel and four-track tape machines. Today, this format is regarded as obsolete.
(*Studio Photocraft/ David Worsley*)

Lower High Street, 1962. Here we see Clive
Castle selecting an appropriate film from his
extensive range available in the early 1960s.
(*Studio Photocraft/David Worsley*)

Lower High Street, 1962. A female assistant
discussing cameras with a lady customer.
(*Studio Photocraft/David Worsley*)

Lower High Street, 1962. Another
of Photocraft's regular staff,
'troubleshooting' a gentleman's
camera. (*Studio Photocraft/
David Worsley*)

Lower High Street, 1962. These two excellent views show Victor using his faultless and helpful sales pitch to a very keen and inquisitive customer. (*Studio Photocraft/ David Worsley*)

Lower High Street, 1966. A splendid view showing the one-time audio showroom and audio demonstration room located above 40 High Street, which is still used today by Soundcraft Hi-fi. (*Studio Photocraft/David Worsley*)

Lower High Street, 1966. The 1960s-styled showroom above 40 High Street, illustrating the speakers, turntables and audio equipment of the day. (*Studio Photocraft/David Worsley*)

Lower High Street, 1966. Another view showing a selection of turntables and amplifiers. Note the padded door and 1960s styling in this room. (*Studio Photocraft/David Worsley*)

Lower High Street, 1966. One of the many showrooms above 40 High Street. (*Studio Photocraft/David Worsley*)

Lower High Street, 1964. This view shows popular beautician Margaret Whitling with a client at her premises, Salon Margaret, at no. 42a, which was once next door to Photocraft on the upper floor. (*Studio Photocraft/David Worsley*)

Elwick Road, 1963. Queues of Ashfordians and budding amateur photographers are seen here arriving at the Corn Exchange for the Photocraft Colour Show, which no doubt included demonstrations and professional advice. Colour photography was taking off at this time for the domestic photographer, and Photocraft were always on hand with their sound and impartial advice. (*Studio Photocraft/David Worsley*)

Elwick Road, 1963. Scores of locals pile into the main entrance of the Corn Exchange. The popular china, glass and hardware merchant, Ward and Humphries, can be seen on the immediate left. Their premises were actually attached to the Corn Exchange. Ward and Humphries disappeared upon the demolition of the Corn Exchange, which in turn was replaced by new offices for Commercial Union.
(*Studio Photocraft/David Worsley*)

Elwick Road, 1963. A large placard attached to the Corn Exchange advertises the popular event.
(*Studio Photocraft/David Worsley*)

Elwick Road, 1963. Although today there are many female photographers, these women queuing were probably only there to keep their husbands happy! (*Studio Photocraft/ David Worsley*)

Elwick Road, 1963. This fine print taken by Studio Photocraft, depicting the Church of St Mary the Virgin, and accompanied by flowers, was set up to welcome visitors to the show. (*Studio Photocraft/David Worsley*)

Elwick Road, 1963. Photographic orator Victor Mathews talks to a packed Corn Exchange about the advent of and the already popular colour photography. (*Studio Photocraft/ David Worsley*)

3

NO SHORTAGE OF
NOSTALGIA

Upper High Street, 1955. A splendid view showing the heart of the town at a time when pedestrians
had to share the town centre with vehicles, although it is interesting to note the amount of cycles in
use back in 1955. For those who find travelling around the town in a car frustrating nowadays, why
not try the old faithful bicycle? (*Steve Salter Archive*)

Kings Parade, 1959. A particularly rare and splendid view showing the alterations and remodelling of Kings Parade, which had previously been minus its classical columns and picture window. Earlier images show a smaller building attached to this elevation with a pitched roof. For many years this part of the building was used as the chambers of Ashford Urban District Council. The works illustrated also suggest provision for individual shop units, which are common today. The opposite end of this central landmark was the home of Ashford Fire Brigade, together with its horse-drawn appliances, reputed to be one of the earliest brigades in the country. (*Brian Badham/Reflections/Weavers*)

Kings Parade, 1952. This night view, going back several years, shows the familiar landmark prior to its alterations for shop units. Taken by Douglas Weaver, this is one of many night views taken of the town at this time. (*Brian Badham/ Reflections/Weavers*)

Churchyard Passage, 1952. Here we see the town's landmark, the Church of St Mary the Virgin, unusually taken through a window. The window actually belongs to either the Dr Wilks Hall/Ashford Museum or the Ashford Tourist Information next door. Many photographs have been taken over the years from the north and south elevations, but from this direction it is a rarity. (*Brian Badham/Reflections/Weavers*)

Churchyard Passage, 1952. The beautiful church shot was taken from the north, undoubtedly its more photographed elevation. (*Brian Badham/Reflections/Weavers*)

Middle Row, 1952. A sentimental look at this still-quaint area of the town, showing Marjorie Smith's popular needlework shop at nos 10 and 11; George Prentis, wine and spirit merchants, at 57 High Street in the background; and the popular hostelry Man of Kent on the right. Incidentally, at this time in 1952 George Prentis were claiming to be the 'oldest wine merchants in Kent'. Over fifty years later, there are very few older traders left in the town. The popular wine merchant, closed in the 1970s, was replaced for many years by a greengrocer. (*Brian Badham/ Reflections/Weavers*)

Churchyard Passage, 1952. This view gives a strong impression of 'peace and tranquillity' in the town. Today, the largely unchanged passage is perhaps more heavily used than in previous eras. This is one of the very few areas in the town to escape redevelopment plans over the decades. Knowing the reputation of past planners in the town, with their many savage ideas, it is a wonder that these charming gems survived at all. (*Brian Badham/Reflections/Weavers*)

North Street, 1978. It is probable that this view was taken on a Sunday, as the town appears deserted. The popular milliners and costumiers, Ashley Russell Ltd, can be seen on the left at no. 2 with Hobbs Parker estate agents at no. 4 on the extreme left. The yard entrance with closed gates, also on the left, later became a pedestrian walkway to the redeveloped Headley Brothers premises at 46 High Street. For many years there was a chapel belonging to the Headley family behind no. 4, and this was demolished in 1977, so this narrow access was aptly named Chapel Mews, and today provides the rear access to McDonald's restaurant, among other smaller traders. (*Stella Pitt*)

North Street, 1971. Not instantly recognisable, this is North Street when still a through road and prior to a large section of the illustrated properties being renovated and refurbished by Charter Consolidated. Today, the Barclay's Business centre and the *Kent Messenger* offices stand where the parked cars are on the right. (*Howard Green*)

North Street, 1972. Just under a year later, work had begun to dismantle the neighbouring Lord Roberts public house, which sadly did not survive under the council's plans. The ancient hostelry is seen here, stripped of its well-known Kent peg roof tiles, and was demolished shortly afterwards to make way for a service road linking Park Street. The town reeled from regular episodes of 'drastic' action during the 1970s. It makes you wonder what the planners had against licensed premises, as so many were lost (all at once) in the early part of this era. (*Ashford Borough Council*)

West Street, 1970. This recently located rarity shows West Street looking rather sorry for itself, only months before the illustrated terraces were demolished for phase one of the ring road scheme, although the opposite side of this once close-knit street still survives in 2009. Many will remember in recent years the sharp bend (near the telephone exchange) that replaced these once residential dwellings. (*Steve Salter Archive*)

Lower High Street, 1963. A magnificent view of the Lower High Street, illustrating many of the everyday businesses of the past. The one-time Odeon Cinema can be seen on the right, which later became a Top Rank bingo hall in 1976. In this view, one of the films advertised is *Middle of the Night* starring Kim Novak and Fredric March. The popular venue had originally opened in 1936, and the decision to change its use was met with much opposition. Midland Bank can be seen next door at no. 39, together with quality grocer G.V. Crump at no. 41. Still spoken of today, 'Crump's' were a must for scores of housewives for over forty years in the town until they finally closed at the end of the 1960s. Another of the popular grocers in the town, Headley can be seen opposite (left) at no. 46, which closed in 1976. Upon closer inspection, many of the one-time businesses that once graced the High Street can be seen, bringing those memories flooding back. (*Studio Photocraft/David Worsley*)

Lower High Street, 1960. At the time of this photograph, nos 25a and 27 were, for many years, the Kent County Council Building Department, to the left and the Welfare Food Office, to the right – the latter was approximately where Gizzi's was later built. Today, this beautiful building has been extensively refurbished, and is now the home of popular bed and breakfast Cornerstone. Now owned by Café Express owner Ufuk Shen, during the sixteenth century nos 25a and 27 had been a hostelry named The Chequers. (*Brian Badham/Reflections/Weavers*)

Lower High Street, 1970. It was approximately thirty-four years ago that Ashford lost one of its last remaining old-fashioned grocers in the town. C.F. Hutson's, illustrated here at no. 19, was latterly run by one of the younger generations of the family. Mr A.G. Morris ran the long-established firm in its last twenty years until its closure in 1974. It was a sad day for the town. Only months later, the former grocers was transformed into Ashford's first Wimpy Bar, and also the town's first fast-food outlet.
(*Steve Salter Archive*)

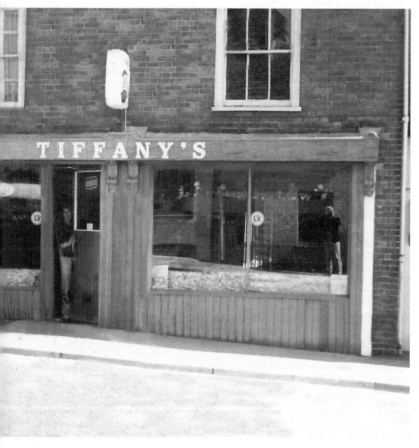

Station Road, 1965. A special treat for those Ashfordians who were teenagers in the late 1960s and early 1970s, and perhaps still celebrate their youth. Tiffany's café will always be remembered by the youngsters of that era, as a meeting point, for its atmosphere, but most of all for its proprietress, Ethel Ayres. Even today, the most senior of Ashford businessmen affectionately refer to her as simply 'Ethel', and one anonymous current-day estate agent claimed that Ethel was a lady to confide in, and a lot of the youngsters used to talk to the popular proprietress, asking her for advice and telling her of their problems. Sadly, the thriving café closed in 1969, when this and the adjacent properties were demolished for the ring road project.
(*Beryl and George Ayres*)

Station Road, 1965. This classic interior view shows the unforgettable Ethel Ayres while serving a female customer at 3 Station Road. Ethel's gentlemanly son, George, has operated as a reputable electrician for over thirty years in the town. (*Beryl and George Ayres*)

Station Road, 1964. Those book lovers in the town will remember Ashford's original library, which was situated in a wooden building on the perimeter of the former South Kent College site in Station Road, overlooking Tannery Lane. The current library, which opened in 1966 at Church Road, is soon to be replaced by a state-of-the-art building which will also house local authority services. The dated 1966 building will be demolished to make way for the new premises. (*Reflections/Weavers*)

Edinburgh Road, 1972. In the years prior to redevelopment, Edinburgh Road was a street largely made up of residential properties and, before it was broken up for the ring road, it ran from Park Street to Albert Road. In this view, we see the premises of N. Lambert, wholesale grocer, stretching from the corner of Edinburgh Road and Park Street. The white-fronted terraced property to the right was, for many years, the business premises of Philip Dormer, chiropodist. The late Mr Dormer was regarded as an acknowledged authority on the history of Eastwell Park, and he compiled an informative book about the subject. By the late 1970s the street had fallen into dereliction, and the site was redeveloped for the Park Mall shopping centre in 1985. (*Lambert Weston*)

Edinburgh Road, 1970. This view shows the business and residential properties on the opposite side of Edinburgh Road. These, too, were demolished. A Wilkinson superstore and the council multi-storey car park now stand on this site. (*Lambert Weston*)

Edinburgh Road, 1972. Just under a year later, a large section of the residential properties on the right were demolished to make way for the ring road. (*Lambert Weston*)

Edinburgh Road, 1972. Another view showing the opposite end of the street at its junction with Albert Road. Hollington School can be seen on the right in the black and white timbered building. The school closed in the 1990s and its former buildings are now private dwellings. (*Lambert Weston*)

Sturges Road, 1972. This particularly rare view shows Sturges Road at its junction with Kent Avenue. This view is totally obliterated today by the ring road. The bulldozed site (centre) was for many years the business of O.I. Snashall, baker, at 85 Kent Avenue. The familiar bakery suffered during the Second World War, resulting in a direct hit and loss of life. The automotive workshops of Caffyns Garage can be seen beyond the site, and were demolished in the late 1990s to make way for a new shopping development on the site. The street is barely in existence today, and is reputed to have been named after Henry Sturges Pledge, the well-known Ashford flour miller. (*Lambert Weston*)

Wolseley Road, 1972. Looking more like a bomb site, this view shows the rear of already derelict and somewhat doomed properties in Wolseley Road. The ring road now passes through where these properties once stood. (*Lambert Weston*)

Wolseley Road, 1977. The one-time popular Saracens Garage, for many years owned by Cllr Harry Lavender and his much-respected wife, Gloria, is seen here in its second location in the town. Previously located in Park Street behind the George Hotel, for many years they also ran the popular Lavender's Bed and Breakfast at the corner of Hardinge Road and Canterbury Road. Gloria continued to run the B&B long after the untimely death of Harry, until the 1990s. Still a much-loved figure in the town, Gloria is seen standing outside the garage at 13 Wolseley Road. The garage had to move again in the early 1980s to Victoria Crescent, upon acquisition of the town centre site for redevelopment. Gloria is more recently known for her tireless work in the Ashford Twinning Association with Hopewell, Virginia, and Bad Münstereifel, Germany. (*Alan Lavender*)

East Hill, 1973. Nowadays, East Hill is predominantly a school thoroughfare, but no longer a through road, as it was here in 1973. Upon the construction of the ring road, it was blocked at its junction with Wellesley Road and Station Road. In 2008, the ancient railings were removed to be replaced by modern traffic railings, causing controversy among those locals who appreciate East Hill as one of the town's largely unspoilt streets. It is still apparent in the minds of many Ashfordians that those responsible for these mindless acts do not know the meaning of heritage. (*Lambert Weston*)

East Hill Mill, 1970. As extensively mentioned in previous volumes, East Hill Mill, which closed as a working mill in 1972, was largely destroyed in a mystery blaze on 16 May 1974. Recently, the following images have come to light that show the familiar landmark before the fire and in its years of dereliction and neglect. In 1981 the remaining buildings were rebuilt to become the district's first nightclub. Today, much of the former mill is still an entertainment venue in the shape of Liquid and Envy, although the upper floors of the six-storey tower have never been utilised. Here we see the white weather-boarded provender mill and barrel-vaulted warehouse, with the sluice gates in the foreground. (*Steve Salter Archive*)

East Hill Mill, 1978. Four years after the devastating blaze, and still registered with land agents, the dereliction has overcome the remaining warehouse and six-storey tower. The dangerous and gutted shell was still an adventure playground for vandals, and no visible effort was made to secure the site. (*Alan Lavender*)

East Hill Mill, 1978. As a working mill the site had substantial outbuildings, many of which were built at the same time as the tower in 1901. (*Alan Lavender*)

East Hill Mill, 1978. This area was all that remained of the building where the older, provender mill once joined the barrel-vaulted warehouse. The fire-damaged roof covering can be clearly seen. (*Alan Lavender*)

East Hill Mill, 1978. Here we see the sluice gate mechanism which still survives today. (*Alan Lavender*)

East Hill Mill, 1978. The part-demolished outbuildings of the mill, to the rear of the Star public house in East Hill. (*Alan Lavender*)

East Hill Mill, 1978. This view shows the small bridge over the River Stour, with the Star public house beyond the trees on the right. (*Alan Lavender*)

East Hill Mill, 1978. The scarred, burned-out landmark tower showing where the older provender mill stood four years earlier. (*Alan Lavender*)

East Hill Mill, 1978. Corrugated roofing blocks one of the doorways, where the older mill once joined the tower and warehouse. (*Alan Lavender*)

East Hill Mill, 1978. The desolate, unkempt site, which is nowadays more familiarly known as a car park. (*Alan Lavender*)

East Hill Mill, 1978. An excellent view showing the derelict and fire-damaged interior of the tower and the warehouse, which had by this time been open to the elements for just under four years. (*Alan Lavender*)

East Hill Mill, 1978. One of the original mechanical wheels which were once crucial to the milling process up until 1972, when the mill closed. (*Alan Lavender*)

East Hill Mill, 1978. Light pours through the half-moon windows of the former warehouse building. A local graffiti artist obviously still had fond memories of the 1960s, daubing the words 'TEDS ARE COOL' on the wall, which was somewhat outdated by 1978. (*Alan Lavender*)

East Hill Mill, 1978. Although the fire significantly destroyed a lot of the flour mill's original features, many still survived, including this old hoist, which could be found in the main tower. (*Alan Lavender*)

East Hill Mill, 1978. Another of the surviving parts of the mill, showing a type of filling machine. One can imagine rows of sacks lined up ready to take freshly ground flour. (*Alan Lavender*)

East Hill Mill, 1978. Here we see part of the overhang to the rear of the barrel-vaulted warehouse, where sacks of wheat would arrive to be hoisted up into the warehouse, and eventually be ground into flour. (*Alan Lavender*)

East Hill Mill, 1978. The interior of one of the derelict outbuildings. (*Alan Lavender*)

East Hill Mill, 1978. The fire-damaged barrel-vaulted roof, which today covers the Liquid nightclub dance floor. (*Alan Lavender*)

East Hill Mill, 1978. A lone tyre floats towards the fast-flowing waterfall, which runs underneath the East Hill Mill. (*Alan Lavender*)

East Hill Mill, 1978. A splendid view revealing the largely derelict flour mill, with the familiar H.S. Pledge name adorning the highest point. The landmark tower was built in 1901. (*Alan Lavender*)

Tannery Lane, 1975. In the days before the construction of the Stour Centre, the only leisure facilities in the town centre consisted of the popular open-air swimming baths in Beaver Road. A decision was made in the early 1970s to build a then state-of-the-art complex on the floodplain alongside the River Stour. The centre opened on 15 February 1975. In 2007 the Stour Centre re-opened after a multi-million-pound refurbishment and remodelling of the pool and many of its facilities. The work was originally destined to be done in phases, but phase one was so far over budget and time that funds have yet to be raised to transform the other half of the 1970s complex. (*Kentish Express*)

Tannery Lane, 1975. The first mayor of Ashford on becoming a borough in May 1974, Cllr Peter Boulden, is seen revealing the opening plaque on 15 February 1975. Cllr Boulden had a second term in office as mayor in the 1980s. (*Kentish Express*)

Tannery Lane, 1975. A German folk group serenades Cllr Boulden and his wife, Peggy, at the opening of the Stour Centre. (*Kentish Express*)

Tannery Lane, 1975. Regular users of the leisure complex will remember its many facilities, which included the stylish Leather Bottle bar depicted here. (*Kentish Express*)

Tannery Lane, 1975. The centre is known locally for its multi-purpose halls, which are traditionally used for basketball, tennis and gymnastics. But in this view, the stage and seating are set up for a competition and prize-giving sponsored by the *Kentish Express*. (*Kentish Express*)

Tannery Lane, 1975. An early view showing the typical 1970s-style reception area and mezzanine levels. Flared trousers were in fashion when this picture was taken. (*Steve Salter Archive*)

Tannery Lane, 1975. The popular River Rooms at the Stour Centre. Again multi-purpose, they have been used from exhibitions to conferences, to parties and wedding receptions. In 1985 a Sikh wedding and reception was held in the Thomas Hall and the River Room. Staff at the centre were so excited and unfamiliar with the Sikh custom dress, that many mistook the groom for the bride! Around forty coaches arrived at the venue on the day. (*Steve Salter Archive*)

Tannery Lane, 1975. The familiar eating area and viewing galleries on the upper floor at the Stour Centre. (*Steve Salter Archive*)

Ashford station, *c.* 1960. One of the last views showing the old, individual tunnelled bridge at Ashford station, with the new bridge structure being built alongside. The Victoria Flour Mills, run by H.S. Pledge and built in 1890, can be seen in the background. (*Brian Badham*)

South Eastern Railway line, 1962. Professional photographer Douglas Weaver made many friends over the years as one of the town's premier photographers. Douglas is seen here with long-term friend and enthusiast John Badham of Godinton Road. Their keenness to take pictures from a precarious railway gantry clearly shows their mutual passion for photography. Willesborough can be seen in the background. (*Brian Badham*)

Ashford station, *c.* 1960. In today's safe working practices, health and safety guidelines are strict and are there to protect both the individual and the company concerned. In the days before the Health and Safety at Work Act 1974, railway workers (minus their hard hats and high visibility vests) work at maintaining the tracks adjacent to the old Beaver Road railway bridge. The governing directorate would have kittens if this casual attitude was taken today. (*Brian Badham*)

4

SENTIMENTAL SUBURBIA

Aerial view, 1956. A splendid view showing the Willesborough section of the Ashford bypass, near to where it today joins the A20 and Tesco Extra at Crooksfoot. The housing development (top left), which was later to be known as Foxglove Estate, is still in its early stages, with the Batchelors factory in Willesborough Road also still under construction at the top of the picture. The now-popular Willesborough Windmill, which has recently been restored, can be seen in the centre. The bypass, which was commenced before the war, became the Ashford stage of the M20 motorway in 1983. Many motorists will remember the roundabout (bottom right) which disappeared upon the road's upgrading to a motorway. A partly completed Highfield Estate/Highfield Road can be seen at the bottom of the picture. (*Brian Badham*)

Aerial view, 1956. This view illustrates Willesborough at a time when it was still largely undeveloped. Gladstone Road can be seen at the bottom right of the picture with Twelve Acres, Hunter Avenue, Osborne Road and Albemarle Road illustrated in the centre of the picture. The green open space adjacent to Newtown Road, which runs parallel with the railway, has in recent years been largely consumed by various residential developments. (*Brian Badham*)

Aerial view, 1956. A superb view showing the expanse of the town before the large-scale developments of the 1960s, '70s and '80s commenced. Ashford Market can be clearly seen on the right of the picture, with a complete Godinton Road dominating the bottom quarter from left to right. During the early 1970s the well-known Ashford street was largely bulldozed and obliterated for phase one of the ring road scheme. Only the section between Apsley Street and Cobbs Wood now survives. The bypass can be clearly seen dividing Kennington at the top of the picture. It is interesting to note that unusual loaf-shaped markings in the extreme top of the picture indicates the early stages of house construction in Bybrook Road and Tadworth Road, which had been completed by early 1970. (*Brian Badham*)

Canterbury Road, Ashford, 1955.
This view, taken from a large crane,
shows piling and shuttering for the
A28 Canterbury Road flyover.
(*Brian Badham/Reflections/Weavers*)

Bypass site, 1955. It is hard to believe today that
this stretch of the bypass is actually now part
of Simone Weil Avenue. Amazingly, the second
group of trees on the right survive today. They are
situated behind the Sainsbury's service station.
This photograph was taken from Canterbury
Road. (*Brian Badham/Reflections/Weavers*)

Warren Lane, 1955. A crane lifts reinforced concrete supports over Warren Lane in the last stages of the bypass construction. The bridge underpass is still used today by regular visitors to Warren Lane, by car or by foot. (*Brian Badham/ Reflections/Weavers*)

Ashford bypass, 1957. Local police stand by in this deserted view of the bypass on opening day in July 1957. The farmhouse on the left still exists today, but is overshadowed by the superior Ashford International Hotel, which opened in 1989 and stands approximately where the railings end on the left. In 2007 this top-class hotel was extensively refurbished to a very high standard. (*Brian Badham*)

Victoria Crescent, 1966. Many tradesman in the area will remember the reputable business of Frank Cooper, building materials, a name which disappeared by the early 1970s. It was the same site that well-known local figure Joe Fagg was reputed to have started business at. Nowadays, Travis Perkins of the same trade operates from the site, which could disappear upon the construction of Victoria Way. The rear of the technical college and Pledges Mill can be seen in the background in Victoria Road. (*Bryan Sales*)

Beaver Road, 1966. This wonderful view shows the once-popular Kennetts Newsagent at no. 16, owned by popular proprietress Mrs C.J. Kennett. The shop closed in 1993 and was demolished in 1999, together with the Butchers Hotel and the former Victoria public house. Today the site still awaits redevelopment, and one may wonder why it was demolished at all. The BP garage now stands on the left of the picture. (*Bryan Sales*)

Beaver Road, 1966. Another view showing no. 16 together with Valet Service at no. 14a, both of which were demolished in 1999. (*Bryan Sales*)

Beaver Road, 1966. In the distant days of the swinging sixties, there were many more garage services to choose from, both in the town and on the outskirts. The former premises of County Motors can be seen adjacent to the street lamp on the left, in this view occupied by John Willment (Ashford) Ltd, which was also a dealer of Ford motor cars at this time. Their service department can be seen in the black-fronted premises on the right, which became Ashford's first B&Q supercentre in 1976. Upon the demise of John Willment, their premises on the left became Kwik-Fit Euro in the early 1970s but were subsequently demolished, together with the popular cinema in 1992 for a new road scheme upon the construction of Ashford International station. (*Bryan Sales*)

Lower Denmark Road, 1966. The premises of E.F. Ealham, wholesale newsagents, can be seen here at nos 42–4, situated in this bijoux residential area just a stone's throw from the town centre. (*Bryan Sales*)

Upper Denmark Road, 1966. Many Ashfordians living in the vicinity of Denmark Road still talk of Equity Stores, pictured here at nos 41–3. Corner shops and stores of this era endeavoured to supply their regular customers with their everyday needs, with a view to keeping their loyal custom from the bigger chains that had already started to establish themselves in the town. Equity Stores were not only a grocer but also an off-licence, and the once-familiar corner shop became Glenda's Beehive Stores in the 1970s. (*Bryan Sales*)

Lower Denmark Road junction with Torrington Road, 1966. Still popular over forty years later, here we can see the well-visited Wheatsheaf off-licence at the corner of Lower Denmark Road at no. 66, at the time owned by E.E. Hodges. Today, this is one of the very few independent businesses for alcoholic beverages left in the town. (*Bryan Sales*)

Providence Street junction with Torrington Road, 1966. Another of the many stores in this area, the aptly named Providence Stores is seen at the corner of Providence Street at no. 19. At the time its proprietor was W.J. Fry. In recent years the former stores have been a fish and chip takeaway. (*Bryan Sales*)

Lower Denmark Road, 1966. The premises of F. Turner, tobacconist and general stores at no. 17. (*Bryan Sales*)

Beaver Road. This splendid view shows the once-busy VG Foodstore at nos 232–4, which at the time of this photograph was owned by W.L. Owen. Today, perhaps not instantly recognised, this is the busy takeaway Hong Kong Kitchen, which is said to be the oldest Chinese takeaway in the town – the business is reputed to have opened in 1970. VG were a smaller national chain of grocery store that disappeared in the early 1980s. (*Bryan Sales*)

Beaver Road, 1966. In recent years no. 258 has been the home of the formidable Davies Family Bakery, which is renowned in the area for their delicious cakes and pastries, but back in 1966 many locals remember it being Buckles Bakery, later succeeded by Ashdown Bakery. Davies supply many outside firms, including the cafés in Ashford International station. The familiar trademark 'HOVIS' sign is still in existence today. (*Bryan Sales*)

Gladstone Road, South Willesborough, 1966. Here we see the memorable premises of A. & O. Wakefield at no. 63. Again, this area of the town was once littered with individual shops and stores of all trades. (*Bryan Sales*)

Cudworth Road, 1966. The premises of D. Dawson, confectioner, at no. 141. Originally a terraced house, today it has been converted back into a private dwelling. (*Bryan Sales*)

Brookfield Road, 1952. There are many individuals in the town who have either lived in the town from birth or are newcomers, who may not realise that this rare gem illustrates the 'forde' over the river, where it is reputed that the name of Ashford was derived from. Today, this scene is more familiar as the busy Beaver Lane junction with Brookfield Road, to the rear of Matalan. (*Steve Salter Archive*).

Brookfield Estate, 1966. These newly finished houses were built to meet the ongoing demand for property in the town that had started mainly because of the London Overspill agreement in 1959. It is difficult to pinpoint exactly where these houses are, but their style suggests that this could well be the Weavers Way/Beaver Lane area. (*Bryan Sales*)

Brookfield Estate, 1966. Here we can see some of the terraced-style dwellings that were built at the same time. (*Bryan Sales*)

Brookfield Estate, 1966. It is interesting to note that the open field adjacent to these dwellings appears to be where the substantial Singleton Estate now stands. Those houses in the distance appear to be situated in nearby Great Chart. (*Bryan Sales*)

Brookfield Estate, 1966. These are the stylish detached properties which are still a familiar sight on the estate today. (*Bryan Sales*)

Stanhope Estate, 1966. In the last few years the well-known Stanhope Estate, which is reputed to have been built on a former prisoner of war camp, has been the subject of some exciting and well-deserved redevelopment and revival plans. These dwellings were also built to cope with the influx of city folk moving to the town, and also to replace many of the council properties in the heart of the town that had been earmarked for redevelopment – Hempsted Street, for instance. Here we can see one of the numerous high-rise maisonette blocks which are now destined for demolition. They are deemed to be dated and the local authorities are gradually replacing them with a more modern lower-level scheme. Popular Ward Cllr Palma Laughton has received and deserves much praise for her strenuous efforts on the estate, playing a major part in the realisation of these exciting plans. (*Bryan Sales*)

Stanhope Estate, 1966. A splendid view showing the tenant-based maisonette block at Eastry Close. The grounds of Duncan Bowen School, which opened in 1960, can be seen in the background. Latterly renamed Christ Church School, the original 1960 buildings were all but destroyed in a massive blaze back in 1991. (*Bryan Sales*)

Stanhope Estate, 1966. Building materials still litter the adjacent grounds in this view, showing the maisonette block in Bredgar Close, with the rear of properties in St Stephens Walk just visible in the background. (*Bryan Sales*)

Stanhope Estate, 1966. Under the watchful eye of their mother standing at the door of her property on the right, these two photogenic children halt their play to pose for the photographer. Incidentally, these children would be in their mid-forties today and may well recognise themselves. This is a typical row of the terraced council dwellings still dominant on the estate, although many of them in recent years have been purchased from the council. (*Bryan Sales*)

Stanhope Estate, 1966.
Another view showing
the newly built terraced
properties on the estate.
The houses are surprisingly
spacious, and are praised for
their solid traditional build.
(*Bryan Sales*)

Stanhope Estate, 1966. Landscaping was
clearly on the agenda when this picture
was taken, showing the front of the
properties in Bredgar Close. (*Bryan Sales*)

Stanhope Estate, 1966.
This view shows the rear of
properties and garaging area
in Lynsted Close. (*Bryan Sales*)

Woolreeds Estate, 1966. An unusual view showing the carelessness of vehicle owners, using this area near to St Stephens Walk as a dumping ground. (*Bryan Sales*)

Woolreeds Estate, 1966. Another view of the dumping ground, showing some of the classic cars of the day whose owners also used this piece of waste ground for parking. (*Bryan Sales*)

Henwood Estate, 1966. Perhaps barely recognisable today, this rarity shows the main groundworks and road laying for the now-thriving Henwood Industrial Estate, at the base of Mace Lane and Hythe Road. Reputable vehicle hire firm Kenhire are today the longest serving business on the site, which for many years was the home of major electrical giant Telemecanique, which manufactured high-quality mains electrical switch gear and associated components. These components can be commonly found in electrical wholesalers such as Rexel Senate, Edmundson's or City Electrical Factors, who all trade in and around the town. (*Bryan Sales*)

Henwood Estate, 1966. This classic view shows the concrete road being laid in preparation for vehicular access to the main businesses destined to occupy the site. The premises of N. Russell, Monumental Mason, can just be seen adjacent to the large tree on the right, a trade that disappeared in the mid-1980s. Also on the right, work is well under way on the well-known Rank, Hovis, McDougall factory. It occupied the vast site behind East Hill Mill until the early 1990s when the factory was demolished, and the site was sold for a substantial housing and business development better known today as Mill Court. (*Bryan Sales*)

Hythe Road, 1966. This easily recognisable view shows East Stour Service Station at the junction of Hythe Road, Essella Road and Mabledon Avenue, back in the days when Fina fuel was sold, Green Shield Stamps were popular and the site offered mechanical services. The Fina name disappeared many years ago in favour of Jet, but back in 1992 the long-established garage was demolished to be replaced by a more modern facility, which today includes a Costcutter convenience store rather than a mechanics' workshop. Many will remember the toilet facilities which were underneath the edge of the garage forecourt for a number of years. (*Bryan Sales*)

Hythe Road, 1966. Another classic view of the familiar garage, in the days when the price of fuel was not extortionate. (*Bryan Sales*)

Essella Road, 1966. Once the former home of Ashford football ground, Essella Road also leads to the highly acclaimed North School, which in recent years has been substantially modernised and developed. This view shows the forgotten Essella Stores, which once traded behind the East Stour Service Station. Upon its closure back in the 1970s, for many years it was converted back into a house. Popular ladies' hairdressers Bev and Sue's have occupied the former convenience store for a number of years. (*Bryan Sales*)

Glover Road, 1966. Nowadays, nos 34–6 are the home of reputable repairer T.C. Tyres and Exhausts Ltd, but in this classic view the premises are owned by Ashford Tyre Services Ltd. The site, which is sandwiched between residential dwellings, is reputed to have been a builder's yard in previous years. Romney Road can be seen in the background. (*Bryan Sales*)

Osborne Road junction with Hunter Avenue, 1966. In days gone by, there were a number of convenience stores in close-knit residential streets, and many of them, such as May's Stores, illustrated here, were housed in residential properties. This memorable view shows May's at its corner location at no. 42. The former business premises can still be seen today opposite Launderama in Hunter Avenue, but as with many of these 'front-room' shops, May's was converted back to a house some time ago. (*Bryan Sales*)

Hythe Road junction with Albemarle Road, 1966. The corner premises of F. Newman, confectioner, newsagent and grocer, can be seen here at no. 312 with the premises of the well-established Earl & Co., builder, at no. 314 next door. Like many former builders in the town, Earl's still offer funeral directors services on the site, while no. 312 is a computer repair shop. (*Bryan Sales*)

Albemarle Road junction with Osborne Road, 1966. Perhaps one of the very few long-term businesses left in North Willesborough, the post office at no. 104 at the top of Albemarle Road, at the junction of Osborne Road, is still at the heart of the community forty-two years later. Back then, it was owned by B.A.J. Bedelle. One local taxi driver, who shall remain nameless, boasted that if he picked up a fare from the vicinity of the post office at night and then radioed the destination in to the office, it would set the burglar alarm off at the post office, because of a conflict with the radio frequencies. Rather annoying for the proprietors at the time! (*Bryan Sales*)

Hythe Road junction with Church Road, 1966. Still a buzzing general store and off-licence today, here we can see no. 406 in the days of its former owners, W.H. Gogay. In recent years the national chain Costcutter took over no. 406 and remodelled its shop front. The familiar 'Free Off Licence – Take Courage' sign illustrated still exists today, although some people have a tendency to misinterpret the 'Free' part of the classic sign. (*Bryan Sales*)

Faversham Road, Kennington, 1966. This period view shows the reputable business of Kennedy's Garage, which also accommodated the business of G.F. Adams, spile and hurdle maker, at its rear. The Kennedy family were also responsible for the still-popular rental business Kenhire Ltd, which started at these premises in 1949 and later moved to Henwood. In later years many locals will remember that National fuel was sold from the site, and back in the late 1970s youngsters could buy Smurfs from the shop, which were also available in exchange for fuel. Kennedy's sold out to Northgate Garage in 1983, which over the years held dealerships for Renault, Peugeot and Fiat until its closure in 2006. The derelict garage is currently awaiting its fate and a planning application to build houses expects approval. (*Bryan Sales*)

Opposite, top: Canterbury Road, South Willesborough, 1966. This sentimental view shows not only a now non-existent business, but also the premises itself. J. Brown, tobacconist and greengrocer, seen here at no. 59, are seen in another of the front-room stores on the outskirts of Ashford. In the 1970s, however, this site was bulldozed to be replaced by a detached property, making this view a distant memory. (*Bryan Sales*)

Opposite, bottom: Faversham Road, Kennington, 1966. An exceptional view showing one of the more recent additions of convenience stores. Still popular in the neighbourhood today, here we see no. 57, which was for many years occupied by C.G. Carter, general stores and newsagents, which also had premises further along Faversham Road at no. 167, previously Gibb and Hussey, draper. In the early 1980s no. 57 was taken over by popular couple John and Bella Patel. In 1999 the store was refurbished, but shortly afterwards kindly gentleman John died suddenly, leaving Bella to bring up their children and manage the shop. In a great tribute to her husband's memory, Bella found the strength to carry on the business and still provides the quality service that John laid the foundations for. (*Bryan Sales*)

Faversham Road, Kennington, 1966. In more recent years no. 177 has been known as Knott's Off-Licence, but in this view the popular business was called Terry's Stores, who were grocers as well as an off-licence. Many Kennington residents will remember Knott's long-term proprietor, 'Stan' Knott, whose real name was actually Leonard. Upon his coming of age, his friendly son, Simon, would regularly help out in the shop until Stan retired back in the 1990s. His elder son, Keith, ran the business until 2008. Under new ownership, the business has now acquired the unusual name of Lucky 7. (*Bryan Sales*)

Faversham Road, Kennington, 1966. In 2009, it is totally unheard of to have a drapers shop in Kennington, but forty-three years ago no. 167 was home to a drapery business by the name of Gibb & Hussey, although the Kodak banner on the upper storey gives an impression that other items were available. Kennington residents will remember the two owners that gave the business its name. Elizabeth Gibb and Florence Hussey traded a successful business well into the 1970s, when no. 167 was sold to become Carters Greengrocers. The handsome property is currently the home of a fireplace shop. (*Bryan Sales*)

Faversham Road, Kennington, 1966. Throughout the late 1960s through to the 1980s, Topple's and latterly Walton's did a roaring trade, with much of its custom coming from pupils of the Towers School. In 1966, G. Topple, confectioner and tobacconist, at no. 272 is seen here adjacent to the one-time Shell-Mex filling station, latterly Towers Garage. No. 272 has more recently been a beauty salon and the former garage has been redeveloped to be replaced by charming town houses. (*Bryan Sales*)

The Street, Kennington, 1966. This excellent view creates an insight into the somewhat calmer and trusted 1960s era, illustrating something that is largely unheard of today. It is mainly owing to these changing times that you most certainly would not think of leaving your child outside a shop in a pushchair or pram, as we have previously seen in pictures of the town centre. Here we can see The Stores, Grocers and General Stores at no. 74, then owned by L.J. Watton. The busy shop continued under different owners over the years but closed in 2003 in favour of another beauty salon in Kennington. Just imagine how lucky all those beautiful Kennington women are to have facials and manicures available on their doorstep. (*Bryan Sales*)

Canterbury Road, Kennington, 1966. Still a favourite for locals and passing trade, the Golden Ball is seen here under its long-term livery of Shepherd Neame of Faversham. In past times the popular hostelry ran bat and ball tournaments in its large and charming beer garden. Its close proximity to the A28 Ashford to Canterbury road does not prevent it from attracting a regular and loyal clientele. (*Bryan Sales*)

Rylands Road, Kennington, 1970. Until the early 1960s, this area of Kennington contained orchard fields but, in 1965, Eltham builder J.E. Webb & Son commenced work to build numerous detached, terraced and (shown here) semi-detached houses. These houses, illustrated at the top of Rylands Road opposite the junction of Ashborne Close, were barely three years old when this photograph was taken. The gardens are more or less identical here, but nowadays every house in this particular street has its own individual style of garden. In the months before road adoption the estate was known as Belmont Park, and the name for this particular style of house is called 'The Keston'. (*Steve Salter Archive*)

5

STREETS AHEAD

An aerial view of Hayward's Garage, 1948. This exceptional view shows the one-time established and reputable automotive business of C. Hayward & Son, which dominated New Street for over half a decade. From 1889 Mr Hayward's business expanded from his trademark 'Onward' cycles to general engineering and the repair of motorcycles, and then to the repair of cars. Despite a disastrous blaze in 1914 and a direct hit by a 500kg H.E. bomb in March 1943, by 1950 the firm was employing over 100 men and had some 66,000sq.ft of workshops. The business continued through three generations of Haywards and the established business was sold to Caffyn's in 1967. Today there is nothing left of the extensive premises that once occupied 20–46 New Street. Kent Avenue, Sturges Road and Sussex Avenue can be seen in the background with popular hostelry the New Inn on the right. (*Hayward Archive*)

Aerial view, Hayward's Garage, 1965. Seventeen years later, the business had expanded across the road and the former New Inn has disappeared in the name of progress. It is clear that some alterations had been made with the addition of a new office extension in the centre of the picture. (*Hayward Archive*)

New Street, *c.* 1950. A classic view showing the motorcycle showroom on the left and the car showroom on the right. The buildings adjacent to the telegraph insulators on the roof were demolished in the early 1960s. Note the old-fashioned pumps selling more than one brand of fuel, something unheard of at today's garages. (*Hayward Archive*)

New Street, 1947. This superb view shows Gordon and Charles Hayward with a 1903 Cadillac. (*Hayward Archive*)

New Street, November 1957. The popular Haywards are seen here with an 1899 Star, after its successful run from London to Brighton on 3 November 1957. (*Hayward Archive*)

New Street, 1953. A splendid
view showing a number of
classic cars in the New Street
workshops. On the right, a
police officer observes while
his beloved police car gets the
once over.
(*Hayward Archive/Reflections/
Weavers 1953/2039*)

Corn Exchange, Elwick Road,
c. 1953. Motorcycles, bicycles
and wireless equipment are on
display at the Hayward's stand for
the annual trade fair at the Corn
Exchange. (*Hayward Archive*)

New Street, 27 January 1962.
A wonderful view taken at the
presentation of a new Morris
Mini van to Mr Oliver Weddle,
Ashford Centre organiser
of the Women's Voluntary
Service. The van was used for
the old folks' Meals on Wheels
service. Mrs H.A. Coleman, the
chairman of Ashford Urban
District Council, can be seen
(centre). Note the photogenic
teddy boys on the extreme left
of the picture.
(*Hayward Archive*)

New Street, 27 January 1962. The WVS members gather around as the new van is driven away to be put to good use. (*Hayward Archive*)

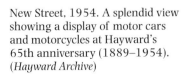

New Street, 1968. Kindly gentleman Charles Hayward shows entrants and customers around a Wolseley Hornet on display as part of the Reveille Paper Competition. (*Hayward Archive*)

New Street, 1954. A splendid view showing a display of motor cars and motorcycles at Hayward's 65th anniversary (1889–1954). (*Hayward Archive*)

New Street, 1957. Hats off! Mrs Mary Evelyn Hayward and Fred Offen with a new Riley 1.5. (*Hayward Archive*)

New Street, *c.* 1950. A splendid view showing Charles Hayward working on an engine in the New Street workshops. (*Hayward Archive*)

New Street, *c.* 1950. Here we can see mechanics working on an Austin motor car and van in the extensive workshops. (*Hayward Archive*)

New Street, *c.* 1950. Axles and other vehicle parts being worked on in the workshops by qualified and apprenticed staff. (*Hayward Archive*)

New Street, 1953. Gordon and Charles with some of their staff and visitors as part of the Riley Service Week. (*Hayward Archive/Reflections/Weavers 53/2043*)

New Street, 1953. Although Hayward's were not a dealer of Rolls-Royce, here we can see great care being taken to clean this classic Silver Shadow, which may have been brought in for service or repair. (*Hayward Archive*)

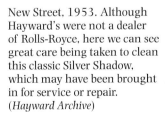

New Street, 1953. A splendid automotive display in the showrooms commemorating the coronation of Queen Elizabeth II in 1953. (*Hayward Archive/Reflections/ Weavers 53/2040*)

New Street, *c.* 1950. Hard at work, the machine shop is busy with the sound of lathes, drills and other precision machinery needed in the automotive business. (*Hayward Archive*)

New Street, 14 May 1957. Charles Hayward presents Mr Percy Kingsmail with a gold wrist watch, after attaining forty years' service to the reputable firm, in the presence of Gordon Hayward and many of Mr Kingsmail's work colleagues. (*Hayward Archive/ Reflections/Weavers 57/1310*)

New Street, 18 May 1953. This magnificent display, showing the bare chassis of a Riley motor car, was on display in conjunction with the Riley Service Week. (*Hayward Archive/Reflections/ Weavers 53/2045*)

Corn Exchange, Elwick Road, *c.* 1950. Another formidable display by Hayward's from the Corn Exchange trade show, with Hercules Bicycles. (*Hayward Archive*)

Corn Exchange, Elwick Road, November 1957. Several years later, at the 1957 trade fair, we see another fine display of Hercules Bicycles. It was bicycles that the Hayward family started business with, long before the advent of the motor car. (*Hayward Archive*)

New Street, *c.* 1960.
Crucial to any automotive
repairer or garage,
the immaculate stores
department can be seen
here. (*Hayward Archive*)

New Street, *c.* 1966.
C.F.B. Hayward looks on
as enthusiasts and visitors
admire a 1925 Baby, driven
by John Coleman and also
advertising the arrival of
Shell fuel at the garage.
(*Hayward Archive*)

New Street, 1950. A splendid
view showing the spares
department at the New Street
premises (*Hayward Archive*)

New Street, 27 February 1957. Film and television star Pearl Hackney talking to J. Offen, chief salesman, at the launch of the new Austin A55 in February 1957. Mrs Hayward can be seen in the background between the two gentlemen. (*Hayward Archive*)

New Street, 27 February 1957. Gordon Hayward talks to film and television star Eric Barker (husband of Pearl Hackney), who is discussing and trying out the new Austin A55. (*Hayward Archive/Reflections/Weavers 53/503*)

New Street, 27 February 1957. Sales staff surround stars Eric Barker and Pearl Hackney, together with Mr A. Good; public relations officer at Lydd-Ferryfield Airport, and Alderman J. Wiles, chairman of Ashford Urban District Council, at the Austin A55 launch. (*Hayward Archive*)

New Street, 27 February 1957.
Pearl Hackney and Eric Barker
stand alongside the new Austin
A55 in the company of Hayward's
staff, local business people and
dignitaries. (*Hayward Archive*)

New Street, 1958.
A sign-written van belonging to
the *Kentish Express* newspaper,
and supplied by Hayward's in
1958. (*Hayward Archive*)

New Street, 1953. This view
illustrates a fine line-up of classic
Wolseley Motor vehicles in the
New Street workshops.
(*Hayward Archive*)

New Street, 18 May 1953. Another view showing local businessmen and dignitaries viewing a Riley chassis at the Riley Service Week in May 1953. (*Hayward Archive*)

New Street, 22 April 1959. This view shows those in attendance for the Riley Dealer Party and the new 4/68 announcement. From left to right: A.B.M. Good, Silver City Airways; J. Offen, Hayward's chief salesman; Charles Hayward and F. Adams, Hayward's salesmen; and representatives from the British Motor Company (BMC). (*Hayward Archive*)

New Street, 1958. For many years, Ashford was host for the Monte Carlo Rally. Being in the automotive trade, the Haywards were involved in a big way, but when the business was sold to Caffyn's in 1957 the new owners did not carry on the tradition. Here we can see a 'Bon Voyage' banner being fixed to the wall of their forecourt opposite. New Rents and Forge Lane are in the background. (*Hayward Archive*)

New Street, 1958. Entrant vehicles stop off at 'Dimmocks Taxi Rank' on the forecourt of Hayward's Garage. Although this is a Douglas Weaver photograph, what is he doing standing behind the taxi rank sign? (*Hayward Archive/Reflections/Weavers*)

Maidstone Road (A20), Hothfield, 1958. The Hothfield Garage of Hayward's, which sets the scene of another stop-off in the 1958 Monte Carlo Rally. Notice the camera crew from the BBC on the right. (*Hayward Archive/Reflections/ Weavers 58/132*)

Maidstone Road (A20), Hothfield, 1958. A closer view showing a BBC cameraman filming the action with supporters and locals standing by on a very cold winter's night. (*Hayward Archive/Reflections/ Weavers 58/134*)

New Street, 1958. Again, photographer Douglas Weaver can be seen at Dimmocks Taxi Rank on the New Street forecourt of Hayward's, alongside entrant no. 314. (*Hayward Archive/Reflections/Weavers 58/135*)

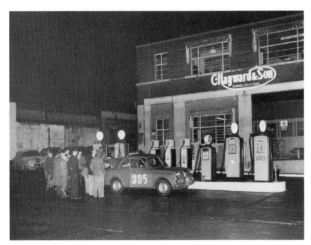

New Street, 1961. Locals gather round to view this Riley 1.5 no. 305 in the 1961 Monte Carlo Rally. (*Hayward Archive*)

New Street, 1961. Gordon Hayward poses with some local rally supporters. (*Hayward Archive*)

New Street, 1961. A mechanic stands by while local people look over no. 305. (*Hayward Archive*)

Maidstone Road (A20), Hothfield, June 1962. Hayward's familiar Hothfield premises are seen here in June 1962. The site has changed hands over the years on numerous occasions. The current owners of the site operate a second-hand vehicle sales business. (*Hayward Archive*)

Maidstone Road (A20), Hothfield, 1958. World-renowned and outstanding BBC motor racing commentator Murray Walker is seen here in his younger days, commentating for the 1958 Monte Carlo Rally at Hothfield. (*Hayward Archive/Reflections/Weavers 58/136*).

Maidstone Road (A20), Hothfield, 1958.
This view shows BBC commentator
Murray Walker interviewing John
Welbrook, the second Englishman
to finish, at thirteenth place, in the
1958 Monte Carlo Rally, driving his
'Standard' no. 173. (*Hayward Archive/*
Reflections/Weavers 58/134)

Maidstone Road (A20), Hothfield, 1958. A
lady cleans the windscreen of no. 145, while
Murray Walker interviews its driver. (*Hayward*
Archive/Reflections/Weavers)

Lower High Street, 23
February 1957. A splendid
view showing the Hayward's
annual dinner and dance
at the today much-altered
County Hotel in the High
Street.
(*Hayward Archive/*
Reflections/
Weavers 56/0528)

Lower High Street, 30 April 1955. Two years previously, the annual dinner was held at the Odeon Ballroom, illustrated here. (*Hayward Archive/Reflections/Weavers*)

High Street (middle), 15 April 1961. This view shows the Hayward's dinner, dance and social evening on 15 April 1961 at the Saracens Head Hotel (demolished in 1965). (*Hayward Archive/Reflections/Weavers 61/1846*)

High Street (middle), 15 April 1961. An excellent view showing members of the Hayward's Social Club committee with (front row) Mr Charles Hayward, Mr Leslie Giles (who received a silver watch for thirty-nine years' service with the firm) and, on the right, Mr Gordon Hayward. (*Hayward Archive*)

New Street, November 1957. Ashford's attractive 'Queen of Light'; Miss Epps, is seen here with the new Riley 1.5 in November 1957. (*Hayward Archive*)

Corn Exchange, Elwick Road, November 1957. Well-known film and television actor Jack Train is seen here together with Miss Epps, Ashford's 'Queen of Light', trying out the latest motorcycles at a trade event that ran from 6–9 November 1957 in the town's popular Corn Exchange. (*Hayward Archive*)

New Street, November 1957. Charles Hayward and Miss Epps pose for photographs on this 1899 Star after it successfully completed the London to Brighton run on 3 November 1957. (*Hayward Archive*)

Corn Exchange, Elwick Road, November 1957. An excellent display showing different models of Vespa moped and an Ashford-made Norman motorcycle, which was available from Hayward's New Street base. (*Hayward Archive*)

New Street, 1961. Young students inspect Austin motor vehicle no. 314 in the Monte Carlo Rally of 1961. (*Hayward Archive*)

New Street, 1961. Locals stand around a mechanic working on Austin no. 314.
(*Hayward Archive*)

New Street, 1958. Young spectators look on as this Riley 1.5, no. 305, in the Monte Carlo
Rally is worked on by skilled mechanics. (*Hayward Archive*)

New Street, November 1957. Gordon and Charles are given a lesson in the new Riley 1.5. (*Hayward Archive*)

New Street, 1960. A big favourite and popular car in times past, a rather dirty Austin Cambridge is seen pulling away from the New Street forecourt. It is no. 221 in the 1960 Monte Carlo Rally. (*Hayward Archive*)

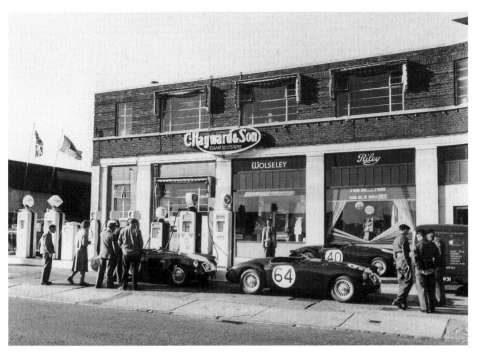

New Street, 4 June 1955. This rarity shows the M.G. Le Mans team refuelling with BP Super at the New Street premises back in June 1955. (*Hayward Archive*)

New Street, 4 June 1955. This classic shows the forecourt attendant filling up Le Mans car no. 64. (*Hayward Archive*)

New Street, 4 June 1955. The forecourt attendant poses with the famous Le Mans Team M.G. (*Hayward Archive*)

New Street, 27 February 1957. This superb view shows married actors Eric Barker and Pearl Hackney alongside the new Austin A55 in the New Street showrooms. (*Hayward Archive*)

New Street, 27 February 1957. A rather serious-looking Mrs Mary Hayward takes her turn in being photographed with the gleaming new A55, with Gordon Hayward on the right. (*Hayward Archive*)

New Street, 27 February 1957. Eric Barker leans on the windscreen, while Pearl and the then chairman of Ashford Urban District Council, Alderman J. Wiles, sample the comfortable interior. (*Hayward Archive*)

New Street, July 1961. Sisters Gillian (left, with the hat) and Valerie Hayward (right) stand outside the new office extension at the New Street premises. (*Hayward Archive*)

New Street, July 1961. This dramatic view shows local firemen taking precautionary measures by hosing down where the workman is drilling to mend a petrol leak. (*Hayward Archive*)

New Street, July 1961. Another view showing work being undertaken to fix the leak. Note the old-fashioned black fireman's helmet, latterly replaced with the bright yellow version that we all know today. (*Hayward Archive*)

Ashford–Bethersden Road (A28), 19 February 1955. An overturned Austin A40 being winched out of a ditch on the A28 by a Hayward's recovery truck. (*Hayward Archive*)

Repton Manor Way, 16 February 1955. The residents of this council property look on in disbelief as a Renault van is winched from the front of their property in Repton Manor Way. (*Hayward Archive*)

Repton Manor Way, 1964. The later recovery set-up of Hayward's included this Land Rover and trailer. (*Hayward Archive*)

New Street, 1964. The recovery line-up just under three years before the business, established in 1899, was sold to Sussex-based firm Caffyn's. (*Hayward Archive*)

Also available fom The History Press

By Steve R. Salter

Changing Ashford

978 0 7509 3714 6

Ashford Then & Now

978 0 7509 3924 9

Ashford 1950–1980

978 0 7509 4223 2

Around Ashford

978 0 7509 4543 1

Kent in Old Photographs

Dave Randle

978 0 7509 4163 1

The Kent Downs

Dan Tuson

978 0 7524 4405 5

Visit our website and discover thousands of other History Press books.
www.thehistorypress.co.uk